SCOUTING
— FOR —
INTANGIBLES

FOSTERING CULTURE
THROUGH INTANGIBLES

RYAN GUENTER

 FriesenPress

Suite 300 - 990 Fort St
Victoria, BC, V8V 3K2
Canada

www.friesenpress.com

ISBN
978-1-5255-9539-4 (Hardcover)
978-1-5255-9538-7 (Paperback)
978-1-5255-9540-0 (eBook)

1. SPORTS & RECREATION, HOCKEY

Distributed to the trade by The Ingram Book Company

For DJ, always.

'As long as you know what you are getting yourselves into'

— unknown junior hockey executive

Table of Contents

SCOUTING

— FOR —

INTANGIBLES

Contextual Introduction

THE ORIGINS OF THIS BOOK BEGAN DURING MY GRADUATE studies at the University of Alberta (U of A) in Edmonton, Alberta. The eventual thesis, titled "Exploring the 'Intangible Player Characteristics' that Junior Hockey Scouts Consider when Evaluating Draft-Eligible Prospects" was defended in 2018. That year, the U of A was the seventh-ranked institution in the world for sport-related graduate research. Readers can find a succinct, made-for-publication version of the final thesis in volume 33, issue 4, of the 2019 edition of *The Sport Psychologist*, under the title "Talent Identification in Youth Ice Hockey: Exploring 'Intangible' Player Characteristics." As such, the foundation of information presented herein relies heavily upon my own research as well as other empirical studies pertaining to talent identification (TiD). The decision to write this book was driven by a desire to share the results without any of the literary restrictions that are required for research and/or publication within an academic journal. In other words, presenting the information in a less formal writing style with the literary freedom to share my own opinion was appealing. I also felt that a simplified version might help solidify some components of the results. The goal from the outset was to provide information intended for young athletes from any sport that hope to be discovered, selected, drafted, or signed. Additionally, parents of young athletes might benefit from information about the scouting process, and the considerations TiD experts use to make final decisions. However, while the supporting evidence was drawn from other team and individual sport research, my own study was conducted specifically within the sport of hockey.

The Canadian Hockey League (CHL) is the largest developmental junior hockey league in the world and is considered to be the primary feeder system to the National Hockey League (NHL), supplying more players to the NHL than any other league in the world. The Western Hockey League is one of three member leagues (along with the Ontario Hockey League [OHL] and Quebec Major Junior Hockey League [QMJHL]) within the Canadian Hockey League (CHL). As such, the three leagues within the CHL contain many of the best junior hockey players, aged 16 to 20 years of age, in the world. Because the CHL is broken down into three geographically based regions across Canada, the WHL drafts and enlists players from the four western provinces in Canada (i.e., British Columbia, Alberta, Saskatchewan, and Manitoba) as well as players from 20 states in the United States. Each team in the WHL is also permitted to have two non-North American players on their rosters; these players are selected through the CHL Import Draft. The WHL currently has 22 member-clubs with 17 based in western Canada: five in British Columbia, five in Alberta, five in Saskatchewan, and two in Manitoba, and five teams located in the U.S. Pacific Northwest. As evidence of the very high calibre of players who compete in the WHL, the recent 2019 NHL draft saw a total of 28 WHL players selected—16 players were selected during the first three rounds, including seven in the first round, five in the second round, and four in the third round (Western Hockey League, 2019). Having scouted within the WHL for over a decade and having the unique experience of producing graduate level research afforded me the opportunity to create this book. While conducting my graduate studies, I was also serving as head scout within the same organization where I began my scouting career as a regional scout. Within the organization, my job was to help the team assess players across the four western Canadian provinces and selected U.S. states and provide input on the identification/selection of prospects that the team would consider at the annual WHL entry draft.

Without ridiculing the actual research results before they are even presented; the simplicity of the intangibles uncovered within the study is worth mentioning. During the period of time that has lapsed since the research was finalized, and especially as I have presented the results to an array of audiences, it has become abundantly clear that the study does not contain any amazing revelations. In fact, the actual intangibles, both good and bad, are very simple. This undercurrent of simplicity might leave young athletes, parents, coaches, and in this case, readers, expecting more. Athletes might hear the intended messages daily and might be inclined to brush off or ignore the results. However, these simple lessons are likely the ones talented athletes reflect upon and say to themselves, "if only I had done ___ or listened to ___, I might have made it!" In fact, speaking with various former NHL players who now have young athletes taking part in the game of hockey, they have retrospectively confirmed that the collective results hold a high degree of accuracy. This is my only cautionary note before we begin: *do not expect to be wowed by the actual intangibles, but do consider the cumulative, long-term intended message.*

Chapter 1
The Challenge

WITHIN THE WORLD OF SPORT LIES AN IMPORTANT ELEMENT that often goes unseen to the casual observant—talent identification (TiD), or more simply, scouting. Before elite players dazzle spectators on the big stage under the bright lights and provide joy or sorrow for loyal fans, they were once just young prospects dreaming of those moments. Scouting may not seem like an overly intricate or difficult task. Find the best players, draft them, sign them, and get them a uniform! However, in many sports, there are normally thousands on thousands of players to identify, evaluate, sort, and eventually select or sign. So, for the unfortunate souls that subject themselves to frozen toes in cold rinks, or travel to remote destinations only to find out a player is injured, the notion that scouting is easy might be a slap in the face. The identification of future potential within sport, and especially youth sport, has historically proven to be a difficult task for not only scouts, but also for those attempting to perfect the art of TiD. In fact, sport researchers from across the globe attempting to solidify the science of talent identification by conducting longitudinal studies (i.e., long-term research tracking athlete development after they have been selected or chosen for certain teams or sports), normally end up with more questions than answers. For example, during a twelve-year research project on youth rugby, Spamer (2009) concluded that "still little is known about a number of variables that could play a role in talent identification, including psychological aspects, diet, role of coaches and parents, and the ability to make the correct decisions during matches." In other words, after 12 years of investigation, Mr. Spamer still had many questions about the factors that might influence individual athlete development, or lack thereof. Therefore, the idea of a "never fail" TiD strategy is, and likely always will be, a mere myth.

In addition to the inherent challenges involved with TiD, the task of successfully identifying and selecting players who go on to contribute at the highest level (there is a big difference between finding players who can simply play at the next level and those that make an impact) is an expensive undertaking. Professional teams spend millions of dollars in resources to fund a scouting department and deploy staff members across the globe accordingly. In 2015, a study found one small-market NHL team allocated $2 million (USD) toward its scouting budget (Schuckers & Argeris, 2015). Despite this massive expenditure for a small-market professional team, it is estimated that only 45% of all NHL draftees will ever play a single game in the league. Beyond the sheer cost of fielding a scouting staff, these individuals can have a profound impact on the future of the organization. Choosing one player over another can be the difference between winning or losing a championship, and can also influence an organization's revenue, exposure, and brand. Scouting is difficult, costly, and the process is far from an exact science.

Despite the cost and inherent challenge involved with talent identification, there have been extensive efforts to create a fail-safe method. Experts, researchers, and professional teams have explored, measured, or calculated nearly every possible feature of an athlete to try to perfect the TiD process. A quick, but far from exhaustive, list would include the measurement or assessment of physical, technical, tactical, and psychological characteristics of athletes (Abbott & Collins, 2004; Baker, Schorer, Cobley, Schimmer, & Wattie, 2009; Calder & Durbach, 2015; Elferink-Gemser, Huijgen, Lemmink, & Visscher, 2012; Larkin & O'Connor, 2017; Vaeyans, Lenoir, Williams, & Phillippaerts, 2008; Van Yperen, 2009). Physical attributes including speed, endurance, balance, strength, agility, and motor ability have been considered (Nieuwenhuis, Spamer, & Van Rossum, 2002; Spamer, 2009; Woods, Joyce, & Robertson, 2015), as have kinanthropometric characteristics that measure body shape/size/proportion, body composition, and physical maturation (Nieuwenhuis et al. 2002; Spamer, 2009). Technical and tactical proficiencies including ball/stick handling skills, passing skills, receiving skills, possession/hitting/blocking/scoring statistics by position, and passing/shooting accuracy have also been considered (Nieuwenhuis et al., 2002; Woods et al., 2015). Psychosocial characteristics, including coping styles, goal commitment, coachability, availability, and implementation of social support, resilience, intelligence, and perceptual/tactical decision-making skills have also been assessed for TiD purposes (Holt & Dunn, 2004; Larkin & O'Connor, 2017; Mills, Butt, Maynard, & Harwood, 2012; Van Yperen, 2009; Williams,

2000). Name a strategy, and it has likely been considered, researched, or incorporated into a system to improve the accuracy of selection within TiD. The multitude of attempts that have been made trying to measure or include the correct factors for talent identification purposes are endless. These vast efforts also provide strong evidence of how vital the role of scouting can be in the success or failure of a competitive sport organization.

Clearly, trying to use a single characteristic would be both a naïve, and likely unsuccessful approach to identifying prospects who are expected to succeed at the next level of competition. As a result, many holistic approaches to TiD have evolved by combining one or several physical, technical, tactical, and psychological characteristics of athletes. This combined approach to scouting is generally seen as an optimal way to select the best players in respective sport leagues. However, deciding which of the characteristics to combine for different sports, ages, or maturity level (e.g., physical, emotional, or intellectual) seems to be an endless evolution of trial and error.

Many of the noted physical characteristics that have been considered for scouting athletes can be measured objectively. Similarly, objective test procedures can be used to assess different technical skills within sports (Falk, Lidor, Lander, & Lang, 2004). For example, professional sport leagues have increasingly used scouting combines to gather concrete numbers or statistics on eligible prospects prior to an upcoming draft. Most professional combines are held on an invite-only basis, whereby top prospects are asked to complete several physical tests designed to measure strength, explosiveness, aerobic capacity, agility, etc. Similarly, objective test procedures can be used to assess different technical and tactical skills within different sports. The rising popularity of analytics within sports—from Moneyball metrics in Major League Baseball (MLB) to the Corsi rave within NHL—are a few examples of how an individual player can be measured based on a series of statistical outputs. These metrics are often used to develop a set of standard scores which are thought to help the organization decide or predict whether an athlete has sufficient technical abilities to be a productive or impactful player. Psychological self-report measures can also be used to assess various psychological and motivational characteristics of athletes in the talent identification (TiD) process (Rees et al., 2016). However, ample debate remains between TiD theorists who recommend the use of psychological profiling, and others who have cast doubt upon the ability of psychological measures to successfully predict future performance potential, or discriminate between athletes of different skill and/or maturity levels (Anshel & Lidor, 2012). A wide variety of normative standards have been developed around test scores which are eventually used within different teams and sports. These objective measures are designed to be used during the decision-making process of whether or not an athlete is considered to have the necessary physical, technical, or psychological capabilities to successfully meet the demands of his or her sport at a higher level of competition.

a) Drafting

Within sports that employ a draft process, there is clearly a vast amount of potential information available to decision-makers who determine which athletes are selected and given an opportunity to move on to the next level of competition. A draft is an organized system whereby teams operate under a standard set of rules that outline which players are eligible and available for selection by teams within a specific league (Koz et al., 2012). Each draft system may vary slightly by sport, but normally they are designed with the intention of making the playing/signing rights of athletes fair for all teams who participate in a respective league. In theory, notwithstanding any prior trades that may have changed hands, the teams that finish lower in a league during the previous season can select higher (i.e., draft earlier), and are granted the opportunity to choose the best players available. Conversely, teams finishing higher in the league during the previous season must wait (i.e., draft lower) to select the remaining players available. The underlying logic of a draft is to create some level of competitive parity across teams within a league so that weaker teams have an opportunity to secure the best or most talented players available during that year's draft. In other words, less successful teams can make quicker improvements as they have dibs on the draft picks that might be able to make an impact with those respective teams. The big caveat, as any sports fan will know, is that the top selections are never a sure thing. For example, consider the following example from the NHL:

> An extremely skilled winger, the hottest thing to come
> out of Russia since Alex Ovechkin, and [he] is already

drawing comparisons to the superstar. He showed no signs of a tough adjustment to major junior, becoming just the fifth rookie in fifteen years to earn over one hundred points. Elite skill on offense make up for some defensive shortcomings and size is a factor, though he has at least a year or more to fill out his frame and grow. All in all, a possible future superstar (Aliev, 2012).

This quote provides an opinion about one highly ranked eligible player prior to the 2012 NHL entry draft. This player was eventually chosen as the first overall selection by the Edmonton Oilers—Nail Yakupov—a Russian-born player (i.e., born in the city of Nizhnekamsk, located in the Republic of Tatarstan, Russia), who also happened to be the first Muslim chosen as the top NHL selection. Yakupov made his NHL debut the following season (2012–13), initially proving he had the physical ability to play in the league. However, he never really found his way, playing in parts of six NHL seasons before returning home to play in the highest professional league in Eastern Europe, the Kontinental Hockey League, in 2018. It is always easy to be an expert in retrospect, but many observers, especially Edmonton Oiler fans, and some experts felt that Yakupov may not have been the best first overall choice. Retrospectively and statistically speaking, there are 21 other players, including two players selected in the fourth round, that have played more NHL games than Nail Yakupov since the 2012 draft. As a resident of Edmonton, there are many folks who believe Yakupov, rightly or wrongly, was a straight-up bust as the first overall selection!

On the flip side of that coin are plenty of examples where players selected in later rounds have turned out to be exceptional professional players. For example, the Detroit Red Wings chose two European players outside of the second round during the 1989 NHL entry draft—Nicklas Lidstrom (third round; 53rd overall) and Sergei Federov (fourth round; 74th overall). Both players went on to play a combined total of 2,812 NHL games, winning seven Stanley Cups between them (four for Lidstrom and three for Federov), and were inducted into the 2015 Hockey Hall of Fame class. The astute reader may point out that the NHL was just beginning its expansion into the European talent pool at this time (i.e., the late 80s through early 90s, as the fall of the Berlin Wall was rapidly shifting the political landscape of Eastern

Europe), but the fact of the matter remains: each pick counts, and adjudging talent in any given year is far from an exact science.

Another extraordinary example, albeit in a different sport, was a player that was considered very average from a physical standpoint, but later went on to accomplish unprecedented feats during his career:

> The scouts snickered. They looked at the time again. To this day, the 5.28 second 40-yard dash time is one of the slowest for quarterbacks in the history of the NFL combine. His 24.5-inch vertical leap didn't have them lining up at his door either. He had been a good, but not an outstanding college quarterback, and as far as statistics went, he was far from a sure thing. The New England Patriots used the 199th pick in the NFL draft to select him in the sixth round of the 2000 NFL draft (O'Sullivan, 2017).

This quote provides the bleak description of a draft-eligible player during the 2000 National Football League combine. The player in question, despite his reportedly below average physical features, eventually became the greatest quarterback (QB) and player in National Football League (NFL) history— Tom Brady. Brady being the best NFL player is debatable, but it is hard to overlook the Patriot accomplishments during his career. After starting his professional career as the fourth string QB, Brady clawed his way into the New England Patriots' starting position during the 2001 season. Over the next 20 seasons, Brady led the Patriots to nine Super Bowl appearances (an NFL record), winning six Super Bowls during that span. In his first season after leaving the Patriot's he also won a Super Bowl with the Tampa Bay Buccaneers for a total of seven championships (also an NFL record—the most championships for a single player). The fact that such a historic player, considered physically inferior to his peers, and overlooked multiple times by every team in the 2012 draft, including the Patriots, raises even more questions about the draft process. First and foremost: how and why did this happen? More specifically, how do these highly successful players get over-looked by organizations who often pour millions of dollars into the scouting process? More importantly, do these players possess or not possess any specific attributes that make them more, or less attractive to teams in the draft process? These are a few of the questions that will be explored over the course of this book.

As noted, scouting can be difficult under optimal conditions, but adding the factor of different age groups into the equation can create more complexity to the process. Despite the array of opinions (and there are many!), the WHL is the only major junior league in Canada to conduct a bantam age, or U15, draft. The other two Canadian major junior leagues, the OHL and the QMJHL, hold an annual minor midget, or U16, draft, which renders those clubs an additional full calendar year to evaluate and make draft decisions about prospects. The early work of Barnsley, Thompson, & Barnsley (1985) reveals the effect of how players born in different months can impact the development of athletes—known as the Relative Age Effect (RAE). More specifically, the RAE suggests that children born closer to a critical age cut-off date may have an advantage in both athletic and academic endeavours. For example, the age cut-off in Canadian/U.S. minor hockey is December 31, meaning players born in the first three months of the year may have an advantage over players born in the last three months. The relevance of RAE in this context relates to the full year's difference between the draft format in the West (i.e., WHL) compared to the two major junior leagues in Eastern Canada (i.e., OHL and QMJHL) operate their draft. If several months have proven to make an impact on the development of teenage hockey players, then factoring in the difference of an entire year is a noteworthy consideration as it relates to the scouting and drafting of minor hockey players in the WHL.

Whether an organization and its scouting staff are trying to effectively project how a 14 or 15-year-old athlete will perform at the age of 18 only magnifies the difficulty of making draft decisions, because players are all over the map in terms of maturity. It is inconsequential whether you are considering physical, emotional, or psychological maturity; junior hockey scouting is a challenge. Given the fact that the WHL must make draft decisions earlier than any other league in Canada amplifies that challenge, and was also an underlying motivation for writing this book.

b) Decisions

Clearly there is an indeterminable amount of information that decision-makers in sports that employ a draft process can use to determine which athletes are selected—or not selected—and given an opportunity to play at the next level of competition. Accordingly, the draft process requires said decision-makers to make difficult decisions about selection and/or deselection of athletes. Recent research examined the selection/deselection processes employed by 22 head coaches of different provincial-level youth sport teams in Canada. They found coaches were generally confident in their decisions to select the best or most skilled/talented players, and those that would likely be future contributors on their teams (Neely, Dunn, McHugh & Holt, 2016). However, coaches became less certain about the decisions regarding the final selections of what they referred to as "fringe players." Further, coaches reported that decisions regarding the final choices of fringe players were sometimes based on instincts or intuition around "intangible characteristics." Summing up the difficulty of this selection/deselection decision-making process, Neely et al. (p. 148) quoted the head coach of a provincial-select hockey team who stated:

> You have all the information in front of you and you make a decision and sometimes the decision isn't black and white … I think there's always an element of "am I making the right decision?" I think for the most part you feel it's the right decision, but I think there's always an element of uncertainty, which makes it tough.

These intangible characteristics were not explored in detail during this particular study, but coaches referred to items such as the personality of players, the acceptance of different roles assigned by the coach, and players that might "fit in" with the other members of the team as attributes that helped them decide upon these final selections.

One noteworthy detail from the Neely research as it relates to the exploration of intangibles in talent identification is the admission by coaches of using instincts or intuition when making final decisions about players. Relying solely on intuition or a "gut feeling" might be a risky strategy, especially when making final decisions about players to draft, or not, and is not be recommended. However, intuition has been considered to play a role in decision-making processes within judgement and decision-making literature. Researchers like Betsch (2008) have studied the idea that successful, intuitively driven decision-making requires decision-makers have adequate tacit knowledge, or contextual intelligence. For example, tenured scouts might be able to detect so-called "intangibles" of athletes and use that information to make informed judgements/predictions about the role these characteristics play in determining whether an athlete might, or might not, succeed at the next level of competition. Over time, it is possible that scouts develop knowledge through experiential learning, which involves the process of how encoded information is stored and retrieved from memory. An individual requires sufficient experience to build tacit knowledge, where explicit knowledge is often directed by actuality in terms of fact, theory, or easily accessible items like statistics in sport. Further, explicit knowledge, in some respects, is linked with objective measures because they are determinable, and most importantly, easily accessible. If TiD was strictly based on explicit knowledge, then it would be easy: make every decision based on the biggest, strongest, fastest players with the best statistics or analytics and voilà, the scout's job is done! However, if it were that simple, then a player like Tom Brady may have never been drafted, or even given an opportunity to play at the NFL level.

From my own experience, what happens with the tacit knowledge of a scout, or group of scouts, is that it tends to morph into a form of tribal knowledge or language that each member can understand and refer to as they discuss players. I can recount hundreds of scenarios when the attributes of prospect A reminded the staff member of former player B. Unfortunately, scouting staffs are normally in a state of perpetual change (personnel changes within hockey operations staff happen often, and in the blink of an eye), so this information gradually changes and rarely remains constant. As veteran scouts leave, retire, or get promoted and new scouts come into an organization, it can be difficult to explain or perpetuate the tacit knowledge or the characteristic(s) that helped the staff make a final decision of selecting a player that was later a success. The task of passing on this tribal language will likely depend on the ability of a staff member to clearly articulate the correct information so this vital tacit knowledge that is crucial to the organization can persist over time.

If tacit knowledge, or knowledge built from prior experience, can help with the deliberation of factors when making a final choice regarding player selection, then it might be beneficial to create a systematic way for that knowledge to be better understood. If this tribal tacit knowledge could somehow be "encoded," for lack of a better term, then the value of such knowledge might be preserved and used more effectively. That is, find a valid way to gather, analyze, and contextualize information that might help clarify specific components of the scouting process. By systemizing tacit knowledge, the TiD community could better understand how a player with less than average physical characteristics, as revealed by his combine scores (i.e., objective measurements), can become the greatest QB in the history of the NFL. Conversely, could the Edmonton Oilers have omitted the obvious physical talents of Yakupov, and identified certain personality characteristics that might have cautioned them against selecting him as the first overall selection? Did these two teams, from different sports, see or miss something other organizations did not? What is that some "thing" a player possesses that creates a champion, or, conversely, a bust?

Within the culture of sport, we hear the word "intangible" quite regularly. Popular media frequently refers to a player having intangibles, and loosely implies the player possesses something that makes them unique (Malloy, 2011). For example, in a newspaper article titled "Best NHL draft picks have a certain intangible," written after the 2013 NHL entry draft, the assistant general manager of the Winnipeg Jets—Craig Heisinger—was quoted as saying, "It comes down to things like effort and compete and will. Hockey sense. The outline is the vision, the size, the skating, the strength. The rest of it [the intangibles] is what makes up a hockey player" (Lawless, 2013). An online newspaper article written shortly after the 2012 NFL draft about Robert Griffin III—a Baylor University football player who was drafted second overall and who went on to become the starting quarterback for the Washington Redskins—described him as "A fast runner and polished passer. Griffin could be a game-changer. Smart player with intangibles through the roof" (Wilner, 2012). However, intangibles are rarely defined other than the suggestion of it being some "thing" an athlete has or does not have. Even within sport research literature, there is no operational definition that provides an accurate and full description of the word "intangible" as it relates to an athlete. Notably, the goal of this book was not to create that operational definition, but rather help the research, TiD, athlete, and parent communities better understand intangibles from a scouting perspective.

If decisions about player intangibles are partly being made by intuition, then explaining these intangible characteristics might help evaluators better identify and articulate what these characteristics are (i.e., the systemization of tacit knowledge). Another benefit in providing such information could also be used to educate prospective athletes and those who train them about the importance and development of these characteristics. Further, this might help prospective players' chances of being evaluated positively in future selection processes. This point was emphasized by Holt and Dunn (2004) during their study of talent development among professional youth soccer academy players, noting that athletes must understand "the need to meet coaches' standards and behavioural expectations" if they are to enhance their chances of being selected (or given a contract or a second contract) to play at the next level of competition. In other words, if players understand how they are being assessed, then that information could help their chances of being selected to compete at the next level of competition.

Despite the lack of any operational definition, a number of studies within the TiD sport literature have shed light on some of the so-called "intangible characteristics" that evaluators deem important when assessing the suitability of prospective players for their teams/programs (e.g., Holt & Dunn, 2004; Kavekar & Ford, 2010; Solomon & Rhea, 2008). For example, Solomon and Rhea (2008) interviewed 18 NCAA head coaches from various sport teams to identify the characteristics of athletes that they consider. Further, Solomon and Rhea also wanted to know what items the NCAA coaches were evaluating when they considered the likelihood that a prospective athlete would go on to successfully contribute to their program. The eventual results generated six superordinate themes labeled "personality" and included subthemes that reflected athletes':

- work ethic (e.g., competitiveness)
- team qualities (e.g., role acceptance)
- mental strategies (e.g., ability to handle pressure)

- coachability (e.g., willingness to listen/learn)
- character (e.g., integrity, trust, and honesty)
- confidence

Importantly, Solomon and Rhea concluded that "it is logical that coaches rely on visible physical aspects when scouting and evaluating athletes" (p. 263). However, they also noted "the significance of the [harder-to-see] personality factors and determine methods for identifying those qualities" (p. 264) in the scouting/evaluation process.

During another NCAA study, Kavekar and Ford (2010) interviewed 27 head coaches of Division I softball teams to assess what criteria the coaches used when determining characteristics that might help the player contribute to their programs in the future. Some of the noted intangible characteristics they considered important included, but were not limited to:

- being a team player
- possessing a strong work ethic
- mental toughness
- character and values
- determination
- loyalty
- game sense
- confidence
- leadership

Holt and Dunn (2004) conducted research with international youth soccer players in Canada (*n* = 20), professional youth soccer players in England (*n* = 20), and six English professional youth-academy coaches resulted in psychosocial competencies that were deemed important to success in elite youth soccer. Coaches cited the importance of athletes:

- taking responsibility for their own development;
- conforming to behavioural expectations of the club;
- willingness to make sacrifices (with respect to time spent with family and friends); and
- clear demonstration of commitment to stay motivated and determined.

Collectively, research studies that have asked coaches to identify, describe, and/or rate the evaluation criteria they use to make decisions about the personality characteristics of prospective athletes appear to share similarities, and overlap one another at certain junctures. This previous research also reinforces the position of Solomon (2008) that coaches and selectors should not only consider the physical and/or performance characteristics of athletes, but also the "intangible, psychological qualities" of prospects (p. 522).

In most sport leagues that use a draft system (even within many sports/leagues around the world that do not rely on draft systems), technical directors, managers, or coaches might lend a hand in the identification or selection of players, but the primary responsibility for identifying and contributing to the final decisions on the selection of draft-eligible players often falls on the scouting staff (Malloy, 2011; Morris, 2000; Williams, 2000). Individual scouts are employed by teams to watch draft-eligible players or "draft prospects" throughout the course of a season, or seasons, in various geographic locations. Their job is to pinpoint those players who they think are worthy of drafting and who might be capable of contributing to the organization at the next level of competition. The world of scouting is a difficult one that requires concentration, accuracy, and above all, patience. He or she can spend countless unseen hours travelling to and then sitting/standing in arenas/fields/pitches/diamonds/courts across an array of geographic regions. These countless hours then require reports whereby that information is transformed into a list of potential players that will help shape the future of the organization. Oh, and the scouts get one, maybe two days a year (e.g., draft day, trade deadline, transfer window) to prove their worth. After that day or two, their efforts can only be truly judged years after the decisions have been made. Scouting is a tough gig, but on the other hand, scouts can and probably should be regarded as the content experts in sports that rely upon them to make decisions about potential prospects.

Within hockey literature, there have been several valuable scouting books, including Malloy's *The art of scouting: how the hockey experts really watch the game and decide who makes it*, and Vollman's *Statshot*. However, despite the essential role that scouts play in the TiD process, the scouting world remains somewhat of an unknown mystery within academic literature. More importantly, and surprisingly, no prior research has ever broken down the decision-making criteria that scouts use to evaluate players. This is a point underscored by Tingling (2017) who noted that little is known about the extent to which scouts in the NHL rely upon analytic (i.e., statistical) information or subjective/intuitively based information when making decisions about draft-eligible players. Instead, most TiD research that has focused on the desirable attributes of players/recruits has primarily relied on the views of coaches (e.g., Larkin & O'Connor, 2017; Neely et al., 2016; Solomon, 2008). While most coaches would likely make great scouts, they are normally preoccupied with coaching duties, and have little to no time to properly evaluate potential players—especially in comparison to scouts, who spend an entire year or more watching and creating player evaluations.

This gap in research-driven literature created a unique opportunity and supplied the motivation to strengthen the current information available on scouting. This book was written to further identify evaluative criteria that scouts use to make selection/deselection decisions about draft-eligible players. Specifically, the book was created from my own research, which was a systematic exploration and identification of intangible player characteristics (beyond physical, technical, and tactical abilities) that junior hockey scouts consider when determining the draft-suitability of eligible minor hockey players. The primary questions that guide the exploration within the book are:

1. **How** do junior hockey scouts gather and use intangible player characteristics in making their final decisions about the draft-suitability of draft-eligible players?

2. **What** are the intangible player characteristics that junior hockey scouts consider when evaluating draft-eligible prospects?

3. **Why** are these intangible player characteristics deemed important in the evaluation process?

Obtaining this information will provide scouts, both within hockey and across sports, further insight into how their peers might evaluate prospects. The resulting information could further illuminate intangible player characteristics considered by evaluators when making selection/deselection decisions on eligible athletes. As such, this should also provide valuable information for young players and their parents.

Chapter 2

The Research

A S NOTED, THIS BOOK WAS DESIGNED TO SHARE ANY POTEN-
tial academic, practical, or applied knowledge that junior hockey scouts
possess regarding the talent identification (TiD) process, and specifically
address the *how*, *why*, and *what* questions regarding the intangibles involved
in said process. The goal was to then deliver the resulting information in a
format where players, parents, other scouts, coaches, and organizations could
potentially benefit from the content. The first step in reaching that goal was
having our research accepted by *The Sport Psychologist* (Volume 33: Issue 4,
Dec 2019), making the results more readily available to the global academic
community. However, adhering to rigid research and literary standards for
publication within an academic journal can tend to soak any "fun" out of
the intended message. In other words, the book is an instrument to reach
a broader audience by making the information less academic and slightly
more interesting. That said, there are components of the research that require
further explanation, which brings me to the research stuff, a.k.a. the method
section. Explaining the methodological approach is crucially important in
terms of valid research, but this section can also cause non-academic readers
(and some academics!) to inherently gloss over, skim, and subsequently skip
forward to the results. Like it or not, this is a reality of our fast-paced society:
when reading something of interest, most folks want to get to the point and
figure out what the intended results suggest. That said, it would be extremely
careless to omit details of how the research was conducted, and how the
results were generated.

The exploration of intangible player characteristics that junior hockey
scouts consider when evaluating draft-eligible prospects was a qualitatively
driven study. The easiest way to differentiate between the two types of
research is to remember:

- **quantitative** research starts with a hypothesis and results are proven or
  disproven by numbers, statistics, and correlations;

- **qualitative** research explores words and meanings.

Generally, the data from most qualitative studies are gathered by interview. Depending on the subject matter of the research, the researcher will conduct interviews with a group of participants, and then try to uncover meaning out of the hoards of information created from the interview process. The number of participants in qualitative research can vary, but normally will range anywhere from as few as four or five, and up to 20 in some cases—this directly contrasts with quantitative research standards where the number of participants is usually closer to approximately 100 or more.

Methodologically, a qualitative description was deployed. During this approach, a researcher tries to generate straight answers which identify participants' knowledge about, and perceptions of, a particular phenomenon (e.g., intangibles in talent identification) from a specific group (Holt et al., 2018; Sandelowski, 2010). Once these perceptions and nuggets of knowledge are gathered, the researcher can present the findings in everyday language, similar to the participants' own language (Sandelowski, 2000). This methodology provided the framework for identifying and describing participants' perceptions of intangible player characteristics when determining the draft-suitability of eligible minor hockey players.

a) Interviews

To gather the required data, a standard interview guide (see Appendix A) was created to help ensure a level of consistency in the questions. Using guidelines from Rubin and Rubin (2012), the interview guide began with a brief demographic section, followed by introductory, main, and summary questions. During the interview process, the questions were asked of each participant in as close to the same format and manner as possible, thereby increasing the consistency of answers. Prior to the participant interviews, a fellow student who was a new WHL scout (with less than five years of scouting experience and not otherwise involved in the study) agreed to take part in a pilot interview. The pilot interview served as a test run for the interview guide and helped refine the researchers' interview skills as they related to the content therein (Markula & Silk, 2011). Although the content of the questions did not change after the pilot interview, the order was modified to enhance the logical flow of the interview, specifically regarding the *what*, *why*, and *how* questions in the interview guide. After the interview guide was finalized, it was then time to seek out participants willing to take part in the research. Candidly, my prior scouting experience provided the research team with the fortune and enormous advantage in accessing members of the WHL scouting community willing to participate.

b) Participants

Purposeful sampling was used to recruit individuals thought to have the required knowledge and experience to answer the research questions being investigated (Sandelowski, 2000, 2010). The one caveat for participation in the research was that scouts needed to meet a minimum criterion for inclusion in the study. Specifically, participants needed to be current or former scouts within the WHL and have a minimum of five years of scouting experience in the league. The minimum five years of scouting experience was key for a variety of reasons, the biggest of which was to ensure participants had seen a "full cycle." This is my own term, but the term simply means that an eligible scout would have seen at least one full cycle of a player's junior career. In other words, a scout would have had the opportunity to witness the progression of a group of players (i.e., age group) from their bantam draft year (U15) through their junior career. In many cases, participants had much more than five years of scouting experience, but this minimum standard of criteria was set as a baseline for the proper evaluation of how intangibles might have influenced the development, or lack thereof, of a player's individual progression.

Initially, the research team was targeting a sample size of 15 to 20 participants that would provide enough data to reach an "expanded scope of confidence" (Francis et al., 2010; Malterud, Siersma & Guassora, 2016; Thorne 2016). In the end, 16 participants voluntarily participated in the research. All participants were male and, at the time, were associated with ten different WHL organizations, although several have changed clubs or been promoted since the interviews were conducted. The participants represented a diverse cross-section of positions ranging from area scouts (e.g., responsible for their specific local geographic region) to team general managers that were responsible for the entire organization. Collectively, the participants amassed 265 years of scouting experience, attending approximately 4,880 hockey games per year in person, and had taken part in a total of 171 WHL drafts. Quite obviously, the group of participants represented a truly amazing wealth of knowledge, and the insight that they provided was without question the strength of the entire study. That said, because of my prior and ongoing involvement as a scout within the league, all participants were known to me on a personal and/or professional level. The benefit of these relationships not only allowed me access to the population, but also created an immediate level of trust and rapport that had already been established prior to the research. When a group of people spend countless hours in cold rinks, season after season, it is nearly impossible not to establish a friendly relationship with those individuals that are there slugging it out in the trenches beside you. Even though we all work for different organizations, and effectively work against one another, it is an honour to be a member of the WHL scouting community—especially the group in Edmonton, which is a healthy combination of great human beings and a collection of characters! In a strange way, the research and collection of data was truly a unique opportunity. The experience itself was somewhat of a monumental venture, as we were effectively merging the worlds of scouting and academia for the first time. Importantly, there will never be enough words to describe my gratitude to the participants and the many others who offered to participate if necessary. Again, the genuine strength of the research was the amount and quality of data that was collected during the interview stage.

The next phase was conducting the interview whereby data was collected through face-to-face, semi-structured interviews in locations that were convenient for each scout (e.g., homes, hotel rooms, private locations at hockey arenas). This was an ongoing process that lasted several months, as it took some slick "stickhandling" to arrange and coordinate times based on 16 different participant schedules. On average, the interviews lasted approximately 43 minutes. Each interview was audio recorded, and upon completion the file was sent to a professional transcription service where they transcribed the recordings word for word, letter by letter. Upon receipt, the transcription files were immediately checked against the audio files to ensure a level of accuracy. To ensure anonymity, each participant was assigned an identification tag (e.g., S1 = scout 1; S2 = scout 2, etc.) so that any information within the transcripts that could identify a scout or his organization was removed. Readers will become familiar with these identification tags in the coming chapters, as many great participant quotes are used to support the themes and results of the research. All of this led to the real fun—data analysis! The simple combination of the two words, *data* and *analysis*, may cause a reader to get into the nap position, but the goal is to make it quick, painless, and maybe even interesting. Maybe.

c) Theme Generation

Despite the general tendency of some readers to cringe at the mention of data analysis, it can be a rather enjoyable process within qualitative research. Provided a person is passionate about the content, the data analysis phase can be as though you are unlocking a code to the countless hours of work that had been completed up to that point. To find the 'lock combination', a technique called inductive thematic analysis was used to examine and scour data for any relevant themes therein. Inductive thematic analysis sounds more com-plicated than it is, but the procedure does require a researcher to adhere to certain steps for the process to be effective. The first step of thematic analysis was to completely immerse and familiarize oneself with the data. This meant listening to the audio-taped interviews, reading, and re-reading the interview transcripts, then listening to the tapes - and then, of course, re-re-reading the transcripts again! Next, the participant quotes were grouped together by similar underlying aspects (i.e., themes), and then data was organized into smaller meaning units. By organizing data into smaller units, the hunt for larger (i.e., more encompassing) themes began (Maykut & Morehouse, 1994). For example, three smaller meaning units included pieces of scouts' responses that identified players who had a positive influence on teammates, who put the team's needs ahead of their own personal needs, and who took personal responsibility for their own actions both on and off the ice. These meaning units were subsequently combined into a larger theme that reflected aspects of leadership and being a team player (Braun & Clarke, 2006). Once the larger themes were established (e.g., "leadership/team player" in the above example), they were then given labels or titles that connected them back to the three primary research questions: how scouts gather information about player intangibles, what intangibles are important, and why the intangibles are important to the scouting process. The one challenge with thematic analysis is that it can get a bit chaotic—in one's own head, and when putting the information on paper. To keep the information organized during the process it was important to implement the use of graphical displays and data matrices. During this stage of the analysis, I used several oversized pieces of plain white paper to help increase the organization, comprehension, and construction of appropriate themes from within the data (Verdinelli & Scagnolli, 2013). The finalization of themes took several weeks of discussion with both of my supervising researchers, Dr. John G.H. Dunn and Nicholas L. Holt, who were instrumental during the analysis phase and throughout the entire research process.

After the data analysis was complete, participants were asked to engage in a voluntary member reflection interview (Smith & McGannon, 2017). The member reflection process was less like an interview and more like a general discussion using open dialogue. The member reflection discussion was designed to easily allow participants an opportunity to comment or add insight about the final themes discovered during analysis. All 16 of the original participants were emailed a one-page written summary of the key findings, along with a one-page graphical representation of the first iteration of the main themes that had been identified (see Appendix B). Six of the 16 participants agreed to take part in the follow-up member reflection phone interview, and were invited to discuss whether they could see their own experiences, views, and/or beliefs in the summary of results. Although member reflection interviews were generally casual, each participant was specifically asked to elaborate upon the role that the organizational culture of their respective clubs had upon the identification, assessment, and weighting of intangible characteristics in the player evaluation process. All six scouts seemed to be quite agreeable, and indicated that there were no huge surprises or areas of contention within the one-page summary of results. Further, the six participants suggested that the results provided a good portrayal of their views and experiences of how intangible player characteristics played a role in the evaluation of draft-eligible players. Although no new themes emerged from the new data, the member reflections proved valuable when refining the structure of results and how themes would eventually be presented. Further, these follow-up interviews produced several really insightful quotes that absolutely needed to be included within the results, as they helped further develop and enhance several themes.

d) Rigor

Qualitative studies have historically been criticized for lacking rigor, meaning the validity or reliability of qualitative research can fall short in comparison to quantitative studies (Neergard et al., 2009). For members of the academic community who might disagree with the verbiage about rigor, it is simply a rough translation to emphasize the presumed difference between the two types of research. To address this shortfall in validity, several techniques were implemented to enhance the rigor of our research. Technically speaking, the member reflection interviews outlined above was one technique used to boost rigor. Also, from the start of the project, I personally maintained a reflexive journal that was designed to acknowledge any preconceptions or potential biases related to the project (Fine, Weis, Weseen, & Wong, 2000; Hays, Wood, Dahl, & Kirk-Jenkins, 2016). This was important, given I was somewhat of an insider as a current WHL scout. Consequently, the reflection exercise allowed me to disconnect any preconceived views surrounding the research questions and interpretation of responses.

Another strategy that was effective in enhancing rigor was utilizing the expertise of a peer debriefing activity, which required the participation of a content expert (Hays et al., 2016). The content expert (CE), who had no prior involvement in the study, was asked to examine/critique the results of the thematic analysis. The research team had a list of potential content experts, but having one of the candidates agree to participate was a different story. Fortunately, our first candidate agreed to participate, and we were extremely fortunate that an NHL assistant general manager agreed to be the content expert. The CE had been the top candidate, as he admittedly considered intangible player characteristics when acquiring or drafting players in previous media interviews. The CE had also been well recognized within the professional hockey community as a person who has had considerable success in drafting players that have gone on to help his teams be successful.

Another noteworthy and interesting fact about the CE's path to becoming an NHL executive was that he began his career as an equipment manager. This provided him the opportunity to, in his own words, "understand the game from the ice up, not from the boardroom down."

Prior to our interview, the content expert received the same one-page summary of the results and graphical display (see Appendix B) that had been given to the scouts who had participated in the member reflection interviews. The peer debriefing exercise with the CE followed a similar format as the previous participant interviews—an audio recorded, face-to-face conversation, which lasted just over an hour. The interview was transcribed by the same third-party transcription service that had been used earlier in the study, and select responses (i.e., quotes) from the content expert were included within the results section.

The peer debriefing interview with the content expert was not only highly useful, but it was also a fascinating experience and great opportunity. As readers will see in the following chapters, the CE provided a fresh perspective on several facets of the study, and his honest insight was a great way to further establish the credibility of results. As noted, the methodology applied in academic research can get a bit dry, but they are essential in explaining how the researchers reached the results. At the end of the day, the research team will be forever grateful for the content expert's and participants' time during the interview stage. Each person provided candid, interesting, and insightful data, which led to some fascinating findings that will be explored further in the following chapters.

Chapter 3
Findings

THE DATA COLLECTED FROM **16** PARTICIPANT INTERVIEWS AND our content expert generated an enormous amount of information to examine—in total, 260 pages of transcribed interview notes! Data was then analyzed, organized, and labelled according to three overarching research questions:

1. How do junior hockey scouts gather and use intangible player characteristics in making their final decisions about the draft-suitability of draft-eligible players?

2. What are the intangible player characteristics that junior hockey scouts consider when evaluating draft-eligible prospects?

3. Why are these intangible player characteristics deemed important in the evaluation process?

The 260 pages of raw data and subsequent analysis created six major themes labelled:

1. playing ability
2. the investigative process
3. desirable intangibles that enhance draft status
4. undesirable intangibles that diminish draft status
5. "The List"
6. organizational culture

Each of the six themes will be examined over the next several chapters, supplemented by plenty of great participant quotes to add value and colour to the information. The themes were chosen based on the merit that they best represented the underlying process by which draft-eligible prospects are physically evaluated, and according to intangible characteristics that junior hockey scouts consider throughout that entire process. It is particularly important to make the distinction between the presentation of the themes in this book in comparison to how they were presented in my graduate thesis. As noted, for qualitative research to be effective, the researcher is encouraged to be mindful of not imposing his or her personal preconceptions, potential biases, or opinions onto the project in question. Academic research results should not be tainted, biased, or influenced by the researcher, which is why the reflexive journal was effective during the interview stage of the study. The reflexive journal basically kept me honest by providing an opportunity to quickly reflect and remove any personal inflections I might have been interjecting during any interview. This is completely understandable for research purposes, and something I needed to strictly adhere to during the process, especially considering my direct and ongoing involvement within the WHL scouting community. However, in a book format it only seems sensible to share my own thoughts and opinions regarding each of the themes that were discovered. That said, I will provide my own take on many of the themes within the book.

The Outline

According to each scout, before intangible player characteristics were even considered, prospects had to demonstrate the physical, technical, and/or tactical abilities to play at the next level of competition (i.e., the WHL). This is the stark reality of scouting—a prospect absolutely needs to have a baseline, or minimum standard of physical ability, that shows he has the "tools" to play at the next level before a scout will spend time investigating the intangibles of a player. While it might be idealistic to only choose players with the best intangibles, it is also not realistic. A team constructed strictly on intangibles, but lacking ability, might field a great group of people but would not win many games in the process. This leads to another blatant reality of scouting—it is a results-based business, and a team needs good players to win games. This is rule number one: find prospects that demonstrate an adequate or exceeding level of ability; then the focus can shift toward the evaluation and consideration of intangibles.

At the start of each season, teams start to identify and build reports on eligible players that have the necessary playing/physical abilities according to the organization's standards. As teams compile more and more reports on prospects that they feel have the appropriate physical abilities, they then begin "the investigative process." The investigative process theme provides a summary and outline of how scouts gather information about prospects and their subsequent intangible characteristics (i.e., sources of information scouts use to evaluate players). For young players and families, especially those who have never been exposed to the intensity surrounding the scouting or draft process, this is often a revealing part of the book. Most teams will utilize different strategies to collect information, but the goal of the investigative process is to learn more about the players, and specifically their intangibles.

A unique feature of the research was that the resulting intangible characteristics were divided into two clear and opposing themes:

- **desirable** intangibles that enhanced the draft status of players, which included four primary sub-themes labelled compete, character, leadership/team player, and passion; and
- **undesirable** intangibles that diminished the draft status of players, which included four primary sub-themes labelled lack of enhancers, body language, selfish tendencies, and parental behaviour.

As the season wore on, scouts would still monitor playing ability, but the intangibles of draft prospects were then considered and factored into a document called the "list." The list is a coveted file created by each team that rank-orders each eligible prospect (e.g., the number-one ranked player being the most desirable draft prospect for each respective club, then the second, then third, etc.). The list is the culmination of the entire scouting staff's efforts over the course of a season and can range from approximately 100 to as many as 500 player names—this is out of the thousands of draft-eligible players that the entire organization and scouting staff will have seen during any given draft/birth year. Generally, the finalization of the list happens in a "war room" type of setting, where all the key decisions makers of the organization are present.

The final theme from the results suggested that teams would refer to the current organizational culture of their respective club as a guide to assess and weigh the intangible characteristics of each player. The organizational culture answered the question of why intangible player characteristics were an important component of the overall scouting and evaluation process. Organizational culture also had an influence on which intangible characteristics were deemed most important to an individual scout or staff when investigating the "person behind the player"—much more on this later. The above outline offers a simplified glimpse into the next few chapters whereby each theme will be discussed in greater detail using an arsenal of quality participant quotes. I will additionally emphasize several themes by adding an opinion or relevant story from my personal scouting, educational, or playing experience.

Chapter 4

Playing Ability

"Talent you have naturally. Skill is only developed through hours and hours of beating on your craft."

— Will Smith

T HE SIGNIFICANCE OF PHYSICAL ABILITY WAS UNDERSCORED BY the fact that all 16 participants mentioned the importance of assessing the playing ability of draft prospects. This process begins every Fall (under 'normal' circumstances) as junior scouting staffs begin monitoring the new crop of draft-eligible players. Depending on the position of the scout within their respective WHL organization, they begin scouting at the local level and then gradually branch out into the major bantam (U15) tournaments (e.g., Rocky Mountain Classic, Calgary, AB; John Reid Memorial Tournament, St. Albert, AB) held throughout Western Canada each season. From my own personal experience, watching a prospect in a highly competitive game or situation is most useful. For example, the quarter- and semi-final games of tournaments allow you to see multiple prospects and how they respond to the intensity and pressure of these moments. Of course, later in the season, any kind of playoff scenario where the season is "on the line" can also be extremely valuable. I recall meeting a long-time NHL scout during my early scouting days and asking if he had any advice to offer. His reply was simple: "Watch who shows up in the big moment." Scout 1 (S1) provided a great quote expanding on this sentiment of watching prospects in the big moment:

> Especially in big time, in big situations, important situations. [He] might not always have the best skill, [he] might not always be the best skater, but you know ... in a game where he's the tenth-best player in terms of skill you notice him more than other guys just because the kid works his balls off and finishes his checks and goes back into his own zone, [he] doesn't just play in the offensive zone.

In any event, scouts begin the process of monitoring a new group of prospects during game situations and start to evaluate what was described by S15 as the "obvious characteristics" of a player. In this situation, S15 was referring to playing ability and later went on to clarify, "we look at the obvious stuff. Skating, goal scoring, puck handling; those are the physical [characteristics of] play. Like those are the tangible assets of a hockey player: the obvious stuff."

Similarly, S7 said:

> I mean once you've watched a number of players, you can see their skating and their ability within their peer group as to whether they're above average or below average. Then you can kinda look at their stride and see if you think or feel that that stride is gonna be able to improve or get stronger as they get bigger and stronger.

While playing ability might be obvious for senior scouts, the ability to spot players with genuine ability may not be initially obvious. Developing an "eye," like any other skill, can take some time, especially for those individuals new to the craft of scouting and talent identification (TiD). This development phase of a scout also played a factor in deciding that the minimum requirement of participants be at least five years of WHL scouting experience. This minimum amount of experience was also designed to allow an individual scout to monitor how the playing ability of several different groups of prospects either progressed, stagnated, or in some cases digressed after the bantam (U15) draft. Young players at the U15 level can undergo drastic changes month to month, never mind year to year; sometimes they progress, and in other situations they regress.

My personal advice for an individual who sincerely wants to excel at any endeavour or craft, is to try to learn from past success or failure. Individual scouts and scouting staffs should strive for the highest draft percentage possible (i.e., the number of drafted players that end up playing in the league divided by the prospects chosen in the draft—much like a batting average in baseball), but one of the realities of talent identification is that failure is inevitable. Projecting how a 14-year-old player will develop physically, mentally, emotionally, and perform at age of 18 involves many different variables. How a scout or staff moves past errors, and learns from their "misses" might help increase the drafting percentage, but may also enhance the quality of players joining the organization. The best way to increase the percentage of draft prospects that are able to play at the WHL level is to select players that excel in terms of playing ability, and that inevitably takes some time to spot the actual quality of physical characteristics (i.e., playing ability).

Over the last two decades, hockey has undergone several changes. The alteration that has probably had the biggest impact on the game is the scrutiny over—and increase of infractions called for—obstruction, clutching, or grabbing. These changes were implemented for one reason—to enhance the speed of how the game is played. As a result of these changes, one of, if not the most important physical attributes in the game of hockey today is the ability to skate. The importance of skating ability has become a critical factor in whether a player can play and be effective at the next level (e.g., bantam to midget to junior to pro, etc.). In fact, all 16 participants indicated skating ability as a physical characteristic they closely assessed throughout a season. As such, ranking a prospect's skating is normally the first attribute that a scout zeroes in on. Teams may have different variations in terms of what they evaluate, but often the assessment could include: overall stride, length of stride (e.g., long and powerful vs. short and choppy), speed with and without the puck (e.g., straight lines, laterally), as well as the ability to change speed, stay balanced, overall agility, and edgework. After a prospect's current and projected skating is deemed proficient, scouts then transition to the assessment of other physical abilities. As S7 explained:

> [The] first thing I try to assess is their ability to skate, and if they can skate then I start looking at their ability with the puck, then their ability with the puck while they're skating, and then try to focus in on their ability to make quick decisions, whether it be anticipation or plays with a puck to try and figure out what their hockey sense is.

The insightful quote above reinforces the notion that skating is normally the first test, and pending the projected ability of that attribute, scouts then focus on a player's skill level. The level of skill in the game of hockey today is ridiculously good, and only seems to be increasing over time. Many of my former teammates or classmates have young children playing hockey, and their puck tricks boggle my mind. The result of this steady increase in skill is clearly visible during the NHL playoffs when the best players on the planet are competing at the highest level. Like skating assessments, skill can be evaluated differently. The following list outlines several key assessments:

- the ability to handle the puck with a high level of control/receive and control the puck at top speed;
- accurate shooting and passing skill from a stationary position, but especially while in motion (i.e., at top speed);
- quickness of a player's release when shooting or passing, especially in flight or in tight traffic areas; and
- consistently perform all the above.

As stated by S15 earlier in the chapter, the identification of skating and/ or skill level should gradually become more obvious with scouting experience. The combined abilities of skating and handling the puck with skill have become so crucial that these attributes are normally the first thing a scout will assess. In my own opinion, deficiencies in either skating or skill can often be the difference between being able to play and effectively compete at the next level, or not. The good news for aspiring young hockey players is that both skating and skill are abilities that can improve with consistent effort. While it may take a moment to comprehend, neither of these physical attributes are static, nor do they have a limit. In other words, a young prospect's skill level at age 10 can drastically improve by age 15, just like a fast-skating 10-year-old lacking technique can be a slow player by the age of 15. Further, although some players may have natural talent at an early age, is there such a thing as too good of a skater? Or too skilled of a player? Personally, the concept of physical limits should not exist, especially for young players involved in sport. Some of the best hockey players on the planet (e.g., Connor McDavid, Patrick Kane, and Sidney Crosby), were gifted with natural talent, but they all seem to have one common attribute. That is, they all have a mindset of continuous improvement and have understood from a young age that they can always get better, no matter how good people tell them they are. As stated at the onset of the chapter: *Talent you have naturally. Skill is only developed through hours and hours of beating on your craft.*

"Hockey sense" was the final attribute considered by scouts when evaluating playing ability. The tactical or technical characteristic of hockey sense is considered within playing ability because I feel like an evaluator can only measure this attribute in an actual competitive, regulated, game environment. Veteran scouts may consider hockey sense to be an obvious characteristic, but there are two considerable factors that make hockey sense a more challenging ability to evaluate. The biggest challenge with having to evaluate, measure, or characterize hockey sense is that it can be defined differently from scout to scout and organization to organization. Unlike skating and skill, the definition of hockey sense may be considerably different between scouts, even scouts within the same organization. Personally, the difference of opinion regarding hockey sense usually stems from an individual scout's playing experience. If you have learned the details of the game by watching, then it can be easy to dismiss hockey sense. However, scouts that have learned the game from the ice before observing from the stands might evaluate hockey sense differently. Secondly, hockey sense can and should only be measured after several to multiple viewings. For example, S12 said:

> If he's the kind of guy the coach always wants on the ice, and for good reason, then those are the guys that I think have game sense. Just being in the right spots, right holes, and being able to move properly within those areas.

To properly gauge the items noted by S12, and many other items that hockey sense might include, a proper evaluation may take five-plus games. In my opinion, the primary reason for this is that hockey sense can be impacted by so many external factors that any teenager faces on a daily basis, such as a final exam the next day, financial trouble at home, girlfriend problems, being hampered by coach or a player, being bullied, etc. Point being, hockey sense is an extremely important part of assessing a good prospect, but it may not be as obvious an ability as skating or skill. Some scouts feel it comes down to general intelligence, like S13, who stated:

> The intelligence on the ice, I guess intelligence you can evaluate as a part of hockey sense, but there's more to intelligence off ice [and] on ice. How do you learn? Are you good at school? If you can learn in school, a good junior coach can take you and teach you something.

Personally, I believe hockey sense can involve many different things such as:

- the decisions a player makes with and without the puck;
- the ability to read the flow of the game and respond accordingly;
- situational sense (e.g., regular shift vs. penalty kill vs. power play); and
- being disciplined or undisciplined in the right situation.

There are several key takeaways from this chapter. The overall goal of this book is to explore intangibles of athletes, specifically hockey players. However, as seen in this chapter, a scout must first determine that a prospect demonstrates the required physical, technical, and tactical abilities. As a team or an individual scout accumulates reports on players that have been adjudged to have the necessary playing abilities to compete at the next level of competition, the attention then shifts toward the intangible characteristics of draft prospects. In other words, find players that "fit the bill" in terms of ability (i.e., skating, skill, and hockey sense), and then consider the intangibles.

Chapter 5
The Investigative Process

"People have really gotten comfortable not only sharing more information and different kinds, but more openly and with more people—and that social norm is just something that has evolved over time."

— Mark Zuckerberg

AN INTERESTING ANALOGY BETWEEN SCOUTING AND INVESTI-
gating was uncovered during the interview process when S10 said, "Well it's funny, because in some ways it's almost as if you're conducting a forensic audit of a young man, to be honest with you." Several scouts expanded that opinion, referring to the player evaluation process as an ongoing investigation that lasts an entire season or longer. For example, S4 made the following comments about a prospect that his team had some question marks on: "It's something that we're going to have to do a lot more investigation on throughout the year and figure out who is this kid." During his member reflection interview, S3 added, "You know it's important to do your investigative work, be it what you think is the most important thing for your own hockey club." These comments shed light on the fact that scouting is not refined to only the on-ice evaluation of prospects—there is much more that goes into the evaluation process.

In addition to on-ice observations of prospects during game situations, it became apparent that scouts attained information about draft prospects from a variety of other sources, including formal and informal interviews with players, coaches, and training staff, as well as questionnaire responses and social media (see Table 1). As noted by S15, "You can get information as long as you have a pretty good source somewhere, but you have to find your sources." In Table 1, you can find a summary of the different sources of information scouts use to build the most comprehensive picture of a player. Not every team will use every source listed, and some organizations might use one or a combination of sources, but the graphic provides a comprehensive list of what most teams might be evaluating prior to making decisions about the draft suitability of different eligible players. Table 1 also contains direct quotes from scouts about each source of information that was identified.

Table 1

Sources of Information Used by Scouts to Evaluate Draft Prospects

Source of information	Exemplar quote
On-ice observations of draft prospect at the rink	S10: "Once I've focused in on a player, and when I say focus in on a player I'm talking about his on-ice performance, then I will set about to trying to figure out who that player is as a person."
Formal and informal interviews with coach (or coaches) of the draft-prospect	S11: "A lot of times, you're finding out more about the player through the coach's eyes than you are [when] you're [dealing] directly with the players."
Formal and informal interviews with draft prospect and/or family members	S13: "The interview, just like anything, is to get the understanding of how mature they are, how intelligent they are, and get them thinking about answering."
Informal discussions with the draft prospect's team trainer (i.e., team athletic therapist or physiotherapist)	S1: "Trainers are good because trainers will tell you exactly how that player has treated them or others. And yeah, I think how you treat a trainer tells you a lot about players, as long as it's accurate."
Responses to formal questionnaires sent to draft prospects, their family, and their coaches.	S6: "Our team does a league-approved questionnaire that we send the parents and the coaches just to get a ballpark idea if they're interested in the Western League, how they are in school, stuff like that."
Social media	S3: "Social media is one thing you can gather a lot of information from just by following somebody on Twitter or Instagram, or whatever other social media [platform] you have."

It should come as no surprise to readers that the one source of information that appears to continuously evolve in the collection of information about players is the use of social media. For better or worse, as the world has grown technologically, so too has the array of social media platforms that provide a virtual voice for anyone from anywhere. From MySpace, to Facebook, to blogs, to Twitter, to LinkedIn, to vlogs, to SnapChat, to Instagram, it is unlikely that a person you want to find out more about is not posting something somewhere. Even though this makes me sounds old, this is especially true for the young folks! Speaking with former, and current NHL scouts, most professional teams now employ individuals whose jobs are solely dedicated to monitoring or sourcing information from social media about potential or internal prospects, as well as roster players. Even at the junior level, the importance of social media responsibility is emphasized when young prospects come to their first training camp. The intensity surrounding proper social media etiquette only elevates as prospects become roster players and firmly entrenched members of the organization's brand. A caution for young players: be responsible about what your virtual presence says about you, because once something is posted it can permanently become part of your personal identity.

The content expert noted an additional source that scouts might consider as an effective way to collect information about draft prospects. During the peer briefing interview, the CE pointed out a very easy source of information that often gets overlooked by scouts: watching "priority players" in practice. When asked if he felt anything was missing from the results, the CE asserted, "no factor [i.e., in the results or sources of information in the study] is put on practice, like how the player is when nobody is watching." Candidly, as intuitive as this might be, watching practice is something I might have considered in my prior scouting experience, but had never actually followed up on. As previously noted in the playing ability chapter, my philosophy was to try and watch a prospect in as many critical game situations as possible. Therefore, wanting to see a player "under the bright lights" made practice seem like an irrelevant scouting tool. However, the content expert's explanation made perfect sense—"You can learn more about a player in one practice than you can learn about him in four or five games." The CE further emphasized his point, and felt that failing to watch a prospect in non-game-day settings was a mistake because, "If you don't do those things, and you only see the player for what he is on the ice when he has that game jersey on, I think you miss a lot of stuff."

The content expert then shared a fascinating story about a time when watching a practice helped him make up his mind about a very underrated (undrafted) junior player. Remarkably, this player not only reached the NHL, but later became a fan favourite in the two cities that he played for during his career. After watching said player collect a "Gordie Howe hat trick" (i.e., a goal, an assist, and a fight) during a WHL game, the content expert decided he would watch the team's practice the following day. His purpose that day was to visit members of the team's coaching staff, but also to take another look at the player in question. His description went like this, "[The player] was out there blocking shots on the penalty kill with four or five games left in the season, with nothing at stake!" After watching this player over several seasons and then witnessing his practice habits that day, the CE made his final decision to sign the player to a minor league (professional) contract with an American Hockey League team.

Knowing details about this player's history makes this story even more special, because his career had always been an underdog story. In fact, this player had been cut from several minor hockey teams and went undrafted as a bantam (U15) player in the annual WHL draft. None of these events deterred him. The player did not complain or feel sorry for himself or blame someone because he was passed over—he just kept working hard and playing the game he loved. Personally speaking, the most noteworthy detail about the CE's story is that this player was a handful of games away from finishing his junior career, and likely had no idea what he would do after that. Many young players today want their career to be a straight line from minor hockey to the NHL. The reality, however, is that no matter how talented or smart a player is, there will be adversity to overcome and opportunities that need to be earned. You may never know when those opportunities might arise, but like the player in the CE's story, keep battling, love the hard work, and get better every day, because you never know who is watching. The CE's story provides proof that a single practice can lead to a six-year NHL career—even if it was tragically cut short. Rest in peace, RR.

Chapter 6
Enhancing Intangibles

AS DISCUSSED, JUNIOR HOCKEY SCOUTS WILL OFTEN EMPLOY a variety of sources to collect information about draft-eligible prospects that meet a team's standard level of playing ability. Over the next two chapters, the spotlight will shift to the exploration of which intangible player characteristics scouts are potentially evaluating. Throughout the interview stage and analysis process, it became evident that scouts considered intangible player characteristics in one of two ways: Intangibles that either enhanced or diminished a scout's evaluation, and overall perception of a player. Intangible characteristics that enhanced, or improved, the draft status of players in the eyes of junior hockey scouts will be the primary focus of this chapter. These desirable, or enhancing, intangibles were categorized by four primary sub-themes labelled a) compete, b) character, c) leadership/team player, and d) passion.

a) Compete

"The power of the human will to compete and the drive to excel beyond the body's normal capabilities is most beautifully demonstrated in the arena of sport."

— Aimee Mullins

Within the context of hockey, at least within WHL scouting jargon, the term "compete" can describe several different items, including a player's work ethic, effort, battle and/or determination level, just to name a few. Basically, scouts are looking for players that put forth the consistent effort required to win and/or get better every day. Compete is often an easy thing to say—a young athlete likely hears about the importance of compete or effort or work ethic from either a coach, teacher, or their parents daily. However, as easy as it might be to talk about hard work as the recipe for success, the "do" part of the equation can be a different story. The execution, and perhaps the under-standing, of this intangible often falls way short for many talented youth ath-letes. Throughout my playing and scouting experience, the players that have that "get better each day," or continuous improvement mindset (i.e., growth mindset) are the individuals that normally find ways to succeed over the long term. This is likely a primary explanation as to why scouts feel the intangible of compete is so crucial in the evaluation process. For example, the following quote from S1 illustrates how some organizations prioritize compete over physical skills and even offensive production (e.g., goals, assists, points, etc.):

> We have guys on our team [whose] compete level is exceptional and maybe 20 of their points are just from that compete level, but I'd rather have that guy that scores 30 points less than have the other guy without the passion and the heart that scores 30 points more.

Because compete is such a vital intangible, scouts will examine the small-est of player details to measure and project the consistency of effort they put forth, as noted by S4:

> Some people might think it's meaningless, but when he skated as hard back to the bench [to leave the ice for a line change at the end of a shift] as if he was chasing a loose puck and it was just that hustle and that—but that's the way that he played, he played so hard all the time.

These small details can provide a glimpse into the larger picture of the player. Specifically, these details can help a scout project the long-term compete of a player, and a potential indicator of a prospect's willingness to put forth the necessary effort to improve in all areas of the game. For example, S11 said, "You can have all the skill you want in the world, but if you don't wanna work at it, pretty soon it's gonna catch up to you." This simple quote succinctly sums up why the intangible of compete is important for any young athlete, in any sport. The quote from S11 also indirectly alludes to the idea that somewhere, someone is putting in the work and may eventually take your job—whether that is at the local, junior, national, or professional level.

As previously noted, the intangible of compete is often a characteristic that is either overlooked or misunderstood by highly skilled athletes. In fact, it is likely the most common misconception within youth sport. That is, the difference between talent and skill, as Will Smith once described it (see quote at the onset of Chapter 4), the difference between talent and skill are the hours of beating on your craft (i.e., hours upon hours of hard work and refining your talent). In my own experience, as an athlete and especially now as an evaluator, it is very easy to get enamoured with natural ability. More specifically, young athletes, their parents, coaches, and even scouts can fall into the trap of thinking that talent alone will allow a player to reach their full potential. But genuine compete is not just the work that everyone else puts in during practice or team workouts, but the extra effort an individual puts in beyond the status quo. No matter how you label compete—determination or effort or work ethic—it normally becomes ingrained within the mindset of elite athletes. Researchers might label this as an athlete having a growth mindset, which roughly translates into an individual who believes they can constantly improve through continual effort. However, a growth mindset that is lit by the fire of compete can be something entirely different.

An extremely easy illustration of a professional athlete that epitomized a competitive growth mindset is Michael Jordan (MJ). To categorize MJ as *just* a professional athlete would be a gross understatement. Rather, Jordan was a living legend of sport, and in my humble opinion, one of the greatest athletes in modern history. Being a teenager during the early 90s, it was impossible to ignore the spectacle of Michael Jordan. My thinking at the time was that MJ was just simply better and more talented than any other player that had ever stepped on an NBA court. However, it was only later in life, and specifically during my sport psychology graduate studies, when I really began to understand why Michael Jordan was better than his peers. Yes, he was naturally athletic, but more than that, Jordan was also relentless. Relentless in his desire to get better through consistent hard work on and off the court. Relentless in his fiercely competitive practice habits, and an overall dedication to his craft. In fact, Michael Jordan really became a benchmark in so many different facets of sport psychology for not only his competitiveness, but also for being able to respond to and overcome adversity, for his leadership, his passion, and his supreme ability to focus on execution under the spotlight—the list is endless. My own fascination with Jordan's mental makeup began long before the Netflix documentary, *The Last Dance*, but suffice it to say I truly believe an individual could create an entire sport psychology course from the content therein.

An obvious result of MJ's greatness and influence on the game of basketball was that he became *the* role model for thousands of young basketball players throughout the world. One of those players was a young man from Philadelphia, PA, named Kobe Bryant. It is well known that Kobe was such a talented young player that he was able to transition from his Lower Merion high school team in Philadelphia straight into the NBA. The fact that Kobe was able to make that jump and play in the NBA at the age of 17 obviously meant he was a unique talent at a young age. After his tragic passing in early 2020, I began learning more about Mr. Bryant—a player that also became a massive NBA superstar in his own right. What I learned about Kobe was that he referred to MJ as his "big brother," whereby Jordan became a mentor for Bryant during his career. Without recounting the entire history between the two players and speaking in overgeneralized rhetoric, Kobe took many of MJ's lessons and transformed them into his now infamous Mamba Mentality. The internet contains loads of information on Kobe's Mamba Mentality, but a good starting point is a simple YouTube search, or you can read his book *The Mamba Mentality: How I Play*. The Mamba Mentality (MM) articulates the mindset Bryant developed from a young age and throughout his career, which eventually set him apart from many of his NBA competitors. The MM provides great examples that effectively portray his mindset, and one specific story regarding his compete is worth noting. Despite Kobe being the best player on his Lower Merion high school team, he approached every practice and each game as if he was the 13th player—a player that did not start games and was used only sparingly over the course of a season. In simpler terms, Kobe would convince himself that he needed to outwork every player on the court in any given situation. Instead of giving half effort in practice, or nonchalantly cruising through games, this extremely talented young player wanted to work harder than anyone else day in, day out. In my opinion, Kobe was a perfect illustration of competitive growth mindset.

Of course, both Jordan and Bryant's work ethic became the standard on teams they played for throughout their respective NBA careers. This standard seemed to work as MJ and the Bulls collected a total of six NBA titles, while Bryant and the Lakers were five-time NBA champions. When the top players of any team genuinely lead with the essential intangible of compete, it has a profound influence on the overall success of a team. In team sports such as hockey, compete is an essential intangible for players, and a critical characteristic for team success (i.e., to win), as stated by S14, "If you don't have compete in hockey, you ain't gonna win for one thing. If you don't have the heart to play hockey, you're not gonna win." While the theory behind compete is simple, it can often be the most difficult intangible for young players to consistently embody, especially as players experience success throughout their career. For me, compete is everything.

b) Character

"Sports do not build character. They reveal it."

— John Wooden

The word "character" within a sport context is somewhat problematic, as it can be described and defined in a variety of ways depending on the person making the attempt. Several participants within the research phase made their own attempts at defining character, and while each of the characterizations slightly differed, there were also common threads that will be explored throughout this subchapter.

Scouts in our research used the term "character" in a variety of ways to capture several attributes that reflected an array of social, psychological, emotional, behavioural, and moral characteristics. One specific description of character that stood out was provided by S10, who pointed out that he and his club considered the "player as a person" rather than just the "hockey player." This description suggests that character is portrayed on the ice during games and practice, but it can also be shown in other places, such as the dressing room, the lobby after games, on social media, at school, and even within the community. Additionally, S9 provided his own explanation of character saying, "We use the word character. And sometimes it's overused, but that to me is the big intangible, and the easiest way to describe it is 'who you are in the dark' or who you are when nobody's watching." It might sound harsh, but this particular statement is relevant in a time when many young athletes and young people (man, I sound OLD!) get caught up in maintaining a public or virtual image—their image on the "Gram" or Snapchat or TikTok or on any other social media platform that will always be unfamiliar to me. Character in sport is not an image—instead, character represents the notion of the interconnectedness between an individual's moral virtues, civic consciousness, and intellect in relation to their performance (Lerner et al., 2011). More importantly, youth sport is a great structure for the development of character and who an individual becomes "in the dark" when no one is watching.

Regardless of how an individual scout defined character, it was regarded as a highly valued intangible for players to possess, as noted by S7: "I place as much importance on character as I do the physical attributes." Obviously, S7's statement speaks volumes about the importance character plays in the evaluation process. The importance of character has always been part of the evaluation process in hockey. However, as previously noted, the game of hockey has undergone considerable changes over the last several decades, and as a result so too has the increasing value on finding not only good players, but also good people. In comparing the historic style of play with how the game is played today, there has been a clear change since the turn of the millennium. Specifically, as the speed of hockey has increased, the focus on physicality within the game has significantly decreased. Those familiar with the game and its history will know what this means. For readers unfamiliar with the drastic alterations in style of play, one need not look further than the state of Pennsylvania for evidence of how hockey has changed. First, look at the Philadelphia Flyers (a.k.a., Broadstreet Bullies) of the mid 70s. The Flyers won back-to-back Stanley Cups in 1974 and 1975 through sheer force and intimidation, dashed with a bit of skill—they could literally and physically impose their will over competitors to win hockey games. Just over four decades later and 500 miles east of Philadelphia, the Pittsburgh Penguins won back-to-back Stanley Cup Champions in 2016 and 2017 with great skill, tactical supremacy, and splashes of grit. The contrasting style of each team in this example sheds light upon the changes within the game of hockey, as the two Pennsylvania teams employed entirely opposite strategies to capture Lord

Stanley's Cup. For better or worse, the game of hockey is now played much more politely then it ever has been, and this drastic shift has impacted every facet of the game. The point is that character has always been a big factor in the makeup of a hockey player, and there will always be different variations of how it is ultimately defined. However, as the game evolved and became less focused on physical play, so too has the broader definition of the word "character." That is not to say teams of yesteryear were not looking for good players and people, but the consideration of what character means from the two eras seems vastly different. This commentary on character may seem vague, but the evolution of the game has undoubtedly changed the talent identification process and has also influenced the way scouts measure character. These changes will be discussed in greater detail throughout the chapter and book.

Regardless of these playing style changes within the game, scouts felt that the character of a prospect was a reflection of the person beyond the player. In some cases, scouts were cognizant of bringing in a "good, well-rounded person" into their organization as noted by S10:

> You want to make sure that if you're bringing a player into the organization that he's going to be a very positive ambassador for your team, representing your team in the community in which the team plays in, but you know, the league and whatnot, so I believe you're drafting *more than just hockey players* [emphasis added].

The concept of learning about and drafting well-rounded people was also demonstrated by a prospect's academic performance. For example, S12 said: "I want kids that are good students, that work hard at school. I mean I think that we're just looking for well-rounded individuals now." The development of character is an essential evolution for any young person, but it is particularly important for young athletes, and their parents, to understand the person beyond the player is a breaking point for some organizations. For example, S1 made the point that his organization was willing to pass on highly skilled or productive players (i.e., in terms of the points/goals/assists collected during games) if the scouting staff collectively felt something was amiss in terms of the player's character:

> One of our focuses has always been, we want good people in our organization, so we've had opportunities to take players that are very skilled, or you know are going to give you 60 or 70 points [a season], or whatever, and we've passed them up in the draft because we know that their character is not great.

If you recall from the previous subchapter (Compete) that same scout (S1) also placed more value on compete over point production. This provides concrete evidence that the overall evaluation of character and compete, or lack thereof, can supersede natural talent for some organizations within the WHL. In the case of character, that same evidence was expanded upon by S9 when he described his team's rationale on finding and drafting players with good character: "Number one is your performance as an athlete, but number two, it's your performance as a citizen and your ability to be a good ambassador or role model for that organization." The citizenship of a player is not only important for junior hockey teams, but it is also a strategy of the overarching leagues that govern each organization (e.g., the WHL). Of course, the goal of junior leagues and their teams is to develop hockey players, but they also have a huge interest in the development of future educators, leaders, and contributors within the broader community. To that end, S15 clearly made this distinction by adding, "We're not just in the business of building hockey players, we're developing young men. We're turning boys into men from their 17- to 20-year-old time, so when they leave us, we want them to be ambassadors of our brand." Some scouts suggested that part of the evaluation process might entail predicting whether a prospect had the potential to develop into a "better person" than when a player joined their organization. For example, S1 said: "Like our organization, our GM [General Manager] is adamant that every kid that comes [into] our organization has a good experience and leaves a better person."

While it would be idyllic to think that every junior hockey player is destined for a long and successful professional career, that is not the reality. Many graduating junior players transition into the Canadian University ranks using scholarships made available to them by teams participating in the CHL (i.e., including teams from the WHL, OHL, and QMJHL) which provides them an opportunity to continue playing high-level hockey while they begin their post-secondary education. This might further explain why junior hockey scouts consider character and prospects that have the right attributes to develop into better people, citizens, or future ambassadors of the organization.

The peer debriefing exercise, again, proved valuable as we discussed the intangible of character. However, the content expert shared a slightly different opinion regarding the evaluation of character, or the "person beyond the player," at the professional level. Early in the interview, the CE mentioned that his experience as an equipment manager provided him with a unique perspective:

> You understand what makes good players, and one of the most important things about good players is being a good person, but … in the changing environment that is today's player, I don't think you can singlehandedly dismiss the kid that you don't think is perfect.

An interesting observation from the above comment is the CE's mention of "today's player," which further supports the notion of changes in the game of hockey, but also within prospects and how evaluators have needed to adjust. The CE also made note of a cultural change in the game, saying, "In today's world of hockey, and in general, you have to take kids with less than quality intangibles, because they're good players and if you don't take 'em, somebody else [i.e., another team] is going to." This is a valid argument of the identification and selection of players at any level of hockey or sport. However, the content expert did recognize the importance of enhancing intangibles, but also noted that the final decision may not always be as straightforward as the results of this research suggest: "You need to have guys with the intangibles that support your team and create your culture and build the foundation of your team, but you also have to take the odd dick [i.e., a person with poor character] because he's the best player." This slight change in perspective leads to more questions about potential differences between junior and professional scouting regarding the long-term implications of selecting highly talented players with "less than quality intangibles"—especially in today's game. Does elite talent and skill outweigh poor character at the professional level? Are members of professional teams more mature? Do professional teams have firmly established and more stable cultures than those in junior hockey? The reality is that there might be a multitude of explanations as to why professional teams choose to overlook certain character flaws in favour of a highly talented player. Unfortunately, there is no way for me to justify any of the differences between the two levels, having only scouted junior hockey. Based solely on that experience, and in my opinion, the most plausible explanation as to why junior hockey scouts might consider character more closely comes down to two factors:

1. The limited window in which players are eligible to play junior hockey. At most, a player is eligible for a maximum of five full seasons in junior hockey, which means the culture is in a continuous state of change. This point leads to the second factor:

2. Most young men can range from impressionable to extremely impressionable at age 16 or 17, which means veteran, or older, players will likely have a big influence on the rookie class. What those rookies learn (e.g., normative behaviours, team values, how they were treated as rookies, etc.) will likely be how they act as they become veteran players.

A recent quote provided by a former OHL player during a 2020 CBC interview regarding an unfortunate situation he was placed in might help illuminate this last point:

> When you're young in that league ... you listen to what the older guys tell you. They have power, they rule you, especially guys who are drafted, they're future NHLers and stuff. You do what they tell you. That's all it is (Bueckert, 2020).

Better yet, an example of the continuous cultural change was provided by S9 during his response to the question of why intangibles are important, and it might provide further clarity on both points:

> Because that's how you win championships. I honestly believe that, and I mean in our league the coaching is so good that if we have guys that are going to listen to that

coaching and steer the ship in the right direction, you know even when they get on the ship when they're 16, 17 and they're just passengers, but they're doing it in the proper way where they're pushing hard every night, and by the time they're 18, 19, and 20 and they're leading the ship they have got that culture that you've built within your team, and they're using it to steer in the right direction, and keep the program going so you don't ever have to turn it over. I think that's so valuable.

The connection between culture and intangibles will be further explored in Chapters 9 and 12, but the above quotes suggest that the foundations of culture in sport, and in junior hockey, begin with the players that are brought into the organization. With a small eligibility window, and highly impressionable young athletes, "it doesn't take much more than one or two mistakes if you will—by bringing in the wrong people—that suddenly your culture is at risk," as stated by S10. Further, during his member reflection interview, S1 explained how his team prioritized character as they built their team (i.e., drafting) by saying, "Ideally, when you look up and down your lineup, say three years after a draft or four years after a draft, you wanna see that character in all the guys that made your club." This quote illustrates how the intangible of character will eventually have an influence on the culture of his (S1's) club. Within the research, and throughout the book, it should be noted that there are a multitude of these intersections between themes and intangibles. For example, some qualities of enhancing intangibles can influence and overlap one another as S7 shared his thoughts on character:

Character means different things to different people or different scouts. You know for me its leadership, for me its selflessness, for me it's the ability to do things with the team in mind, and you know off-ice and on-ice leadership to me is the most important thing.

Again, we see another slight variation of how character can be defined, but S7 is clear that his definition includes leadership and selflessness, which perfectly leads the discussion into the next subchapter.

c) Leadership/Team Player

The strength of the team is each individual member.
The strength of each member is the team."

— Phil Jackson

The efficient operation of any business, team, or organization requires strong leadership. It should come as no surprise then that all 16 participants specifically mentioned the importance of draft-eligible prospects providing potential leadership qualities for the organization. Leadership in team sports can be exemplified by a player that has a positive influence on teammates, puts the team's needs ahead of his/her own personal goals, acts as a role model for younger players, and acts responsibly with a high degree of maturity (or character) on and off the ice. At most levels of hockey, including minor hockey, leaders are normally recognized through the allocation of letters assigned to them. In most cases, a team will designate two or three alternate captains (who wear the letter "A" on the upper left side of their jersey), and the team captain (who is assigned the letter "C"). During his interview, S4 stated:

> That's one of the first things that I look for when I'm scouting games, is 'who is the captain, who are the assistants? And who is not?' If it's one of the top [i.e., most skilled] players in the team and they're not wearing a letter, I question why, and that will be one of the questions that I ask the coach.

This is an obvious way to begin the assessment of leadership, but normally it's just the starting point when trying to project the potential leadership qualities of individual prospects. Another tactic to assess leadership is closely monitoring on-ice interactions between the draft prospect, his teammates, and coaches. Scouts will take note of certain overt behaviours which can be seen during games as further evidence, as stated here by S5, "Leadership, how they handle situations on the ice, how they handle their teammates, how they handle their coaches, yeah for sure. I'll report on that stuff anytime I see it, absolutely." S15 also provided details about specific behavioural examples that he felt were indicators of good leadership:

> I was thinking of this one player, just straight-out leadership abilities you could see at 14 [years of age], being the last guy off the ice because he's high-fiving and celebrating every teammate as they go off the ice and being the guy that helps put the pucks away after warm-up.

Scouts also noted that draft prospects who were evaluated as having good leadership potential placed the needs of their team ahead of their own personal needs. Specifically, S10 noted that he sought players who "put the interests of the team ahead of the individual. I'm a firm believer that if the team has success, the individual players will likely succeed as well." In most team sports, a good a leader and team player is synonymous—meaning a player that understands the larger picture and consistently prioritizes the team's needs first will often become a strong leader. S8 further reinforced the importance of being a team player when he stated:

> You have to be a team guy, you have to play for the ultimate goal and that's having success as a team. You have to be a good teammate, you have to be able to participate in a team environment.

Scouts undoubtedly felt strongly about draft prospects with leadership abilities and having a team-first attitude, but they also noted the importance of players being able to fit in and function effectively with their teammates. As noted by S13, "The ability to function within a team atmosphere, to function with all different kinds of characters … And if you can't be a team player, I don't think you can be a success at a team sport."

Ideally, most coaches dream of an entire roster of leaders, and a group of individuals who are willing to put the needs of the team ahead of their own. Before, during, or after many of my research presentations, the following question is frequently asked: "What is the easiest way to get noticed by scouts?" My answer is always the same: win. If you have a group of individuals who are all pulling the proverbial rope in the same direction (i.e., putting the team first), they can accomplish special things and will likely have a chance to win every game. Further, the more a team wins during a season and through-out the playoffs means more eyes are focused on that group of players. In other words, winning often translates into more exposure for *all* players, including those who may not even be draft considerations on a different team, or players being selected higher than they might otherwise be taken. Not only do players receive more exposure by being part of successful teams, they also learn how to win, and my own opinion has always been: winning is never an accident. Once a player understands that it takes an entire team to win, they are more likely to win again during their career. A prime example is Scott Niedermayer, who was a two-time WHL champion (including one Memorial Cup), World Junior champion, four-time Stanley Cup champion, two-time Olympic gold medalist, and World Cup of Hockey champion.

Unfortunately, in "today's game," the concept of team can be secondary to individual achievements. While it likely happens at every level of minor hockey, this individualistic behaviour seems to ramp up and become more pronounced during perceived big seasons, such as the year of the WHL bantam (U15) draft. In this respect, a certain part of me feels as though the game has lost its way on what it means to be a team, and this individual focus starts at a very young age. Whether individualism in hockey is a symptom of the media, social media, messages from home (e.g., parents, grandparents, siblings), society, politics or all of the above, it is a trend that appears to only strengthen over time. A good way to describe this paradigm shift within the junior hockey league is that historically *players* needed to convince an organi-zation how they could add value to the team. Today, the *organization* now has to convince the player how the team can add value for the prospect. Call me an old-timer, but the days of earning your keep are long gone. Perhaps that is why leadership and a team-first attitude are essential intangibles for scouts to consider during the draft evaluation process.

d) Passion

"Passion is kind of an important word for me, whether it's playing sports or whether it's just living or whatever you're going to do. In my opinion you should be passionate about it, or else, why do it?"

— Pat Tillman

In ten of the 16 scout interviews, passion and a genuine love of the game were identified as desirable intangible characteristics they tried to evaluate when observing players. Despite passion being a difficult item to measure, 10 scouts felt it was an important characteristic that enabled players to persevere and overcome challenges at higher levels of competition. Hockey is a sport where players leave their families at a relatively young age (16 years or younger) and a game where the competitive demands (physically, psychologically, emotionally, etc.) continually increase as players advance to higher levels of competition (e.g., from minor hockey to junior hockey to professional hockey). S7 solidified this point by saying, "Well, number one would be passion, because I think without that passion and love of the game, it's a very difficult game to play as you move up to higher levels." Many young athletes involved in sport dream about the fame or notoriety, and potential monetary benefits that come with reaching the professional level. Those perks are great when everything is smooth sailing, but when the boat gets a bit rocky, those dreamy advantages can quickly become demands or scrutiny, and that pressure undoubtedly increases during those times. Metaphorically, passion is an instrument that can keep the boat moving in the right direction.

A player with passion was also seen as an attribute that can create a positive impact upon the organization and/or team environment. S1 stated:

> If a guy is passionate about the game, it translates into all
> parts of his game … and it kind of creates an atmosphere
> in the dressing room and in the organization. To me, that
> passion and drive is something that just trickles down to
> everybody and makes your whole team better.

Similarly, S12 noted that the best players to draft are the ones who are "engaged, passionate, you know, bring people up rather than push people down, those kinda guys."

Another frequently asked questions posed to me during research presentations is, "How do scouts actually measure passion?" That is a completely valid question, as it is tough to measure a person's true passion for any given activity. However, gauging the intangible of passion will normally require a scout to combine what his/her instinct tells them from on-ice viewings (i.e., tacit knowledge), with the investigative information they collect to determine which players genuinely love the game. This is a point S8 made by saying, "How does a player use those skills that he has? Does he really wanna play, does he have the commitment to play?" Even though this method seems a bit like guesswork, if an experienced scout is collecting the right information (i.e., asking the right questions from the right sources) and closely monitoring what a player's body language says over the course of a season, it can be quite accurate in terms of the passion level of a player. Further, the assessment of passion can sometimes be more closely related to the "gut feeling" that a scout develops over time through trial and error rather than a concrete validation.

If an organization were adamant about its scouting staff precisely measuring the intangible of passion, they could also administer Athlete Self-report Measures (ASRM) to prospects prior to an upcoming draft. A few examples of ASRM related to passion might include using Profile of Mood States, Recovery–Stress Questionnaire for Athletes, and Daily Analyses of Life Demands for Athletes (Saw, Main, & Gastin 2015). As noted earlier, the use of psychological measures for talent identification and predicting future performance potential of athletes has been debated on both sides of the coin. Regardless of how an organization or group of scouts measure passion (i.e., the old-school gut feeling vs. ASRM), it appeared to be a legitimate intangible that enabled players to persist during difficult or adverse situations. Every athlete or parent might envision a smooth, straight line from point A to point B during a young player's career, but it is rare that an athlete will not encounter adversity along the way. If passion is a buffer against adversity, and an athlete accepts that he/she is bound to face challenges, then they may be better equipped to handle phases when they might be susceptible to burnout.

Passion in sport, and in life, is a critical element of human motivation. In sport, there are players that might be more interested in the image, or sporting the team jacket, over the actual joy of continuously competing because they love the game and want to get better. That said, most scouts would likely prefer the latter over the player who is only interested in the image, because athletes that truly love what they are doing will normally find a way to continue the journey no matter what obstacles they might have to face.

In my opinion, this is true in sport and life, and why this intangible is so relevant for young athletes to learn. If an athlete is not passionate about the sport they are involved with, they are still learning about the importance of this intangible, and as Pat Tillman said, why would you do anything without passion? Good question.

Chapter 7
Diminishing Intangibles

BASED ON THE COLLECTIVE INSIGHTS PROVIDED BY A CROSS section of junior hockey evaluators, four intangible characteristics were described as enhancing the draft status of eligible prospects. Conversely, junior hockey scouts also revealed several intangible characteristics that diminished the draft status of players. Diminishing intangibles were regarded as those intangible characteristics that made scouts hesitant of drafting a player. Importantly, this is the first research project that has revealed intangibles that detract from the evaluation of a prospect. Prior, intangibles were only categorized or thought of as positive attributes, but the overwhelming evidence presented in this chapter suggests otherwise. Like the desirable attributes, the diminishing-intangibles theme also contained four lower-order themes that were labelled: lack of enhancers, body language, selfish tendencies, and parental behaviour.

a) Lack of Enhancers

> *"If you have good character, you have good leadership, you have a good work ethic. You know that player is going to get better; you know that player will contribute to your program, and you won't find high-skilled players at the bottom of the draft; and if you do, that's a real red flag."*

— Scout 9

Although scouts clearly valued enhancing intangibles, they were also likely to take careful note of players who glaringly lacked any of those positive characteristics. For example, S13 felt that a player lacking compete was unlikely to be successful. "If you don't compete, you can't play. If you don't have the ability to learn new skills to improve to get to the next level, you can't play." As was highlighted in Chapter 6 while discussing the advantages of consistent compete, talent is great to have, but it is never a static physical feature. Despite the common misconception that talent will always reign, it is often the player that is willing to put in extra work that continuously develops skill over the long term. Another key component in gauging this intangible is the consistency of a player's compete, especially at a young age. It is quite reasonable that by watching a bantam player during five separate games or viewings that they will likely show you the consistency of their work ethic during that time frame. If a scout still has questions about the competitive consistency of a prospect, then it is normally very easy to verify during the investigative stage of the process.

Irrespective of how an individual or scouting staff defined character during the evaluation process, a prospect seen as having character flaws would likely have his draft status lowered. For example, S7 described how a skilled player lacking character would likely necessitate lowering his ranking: "I rank my players lower based on if I know of some character flaws, then I would rate the player lower on my list regardless of skill." S13 also added that a player with character flaws, or a lack of leadership, would likely require further consideration and discussion amongst the entire organization's scouting staff:

> If there's a definite character issue in terms of a kid has a problem or could potentially have a problem or makes really poor life choices or is a negative influence on those around him, yeah, those need to come up and they're talked about.

Players lacking the ability to be a good teammate, or those incapable of interacting effectively socially, were also considered as having diminishing intangibles. S12 suggested that prospects lacking these positive qualities was a static characteristic that normally would not change in a player: "I can work with kids on their stick handling, but if a kid doesn't know how to be a [good] teammate, I'm not sure you can teach it." This statement could create further debate, as some individuals believe young players (e.g., the U15 age category) can actively work to become better teammates over time. In other words, in the right environment and under the right guidance, a player can develop the personality skills required to become a better teammate. That said, I do recall speaking "offline" with this particular scout (S12) about his statement, and specifically whether players could change habits to become a better teammate at, or after, the age of 14—the age that players are evaluated and drafted by WHL teams. During this conversation, we both agreed that by the time a player reached his WHL draft season, it would be extremely difficult for them to alter their style as a teammate. If teammate skills are fixed by age 14, then this would emphasize the need to reinforce and teach younger players the benefits of being a good teammate (e.g., the FUNdamental stage which refers to children from ages 6–12 as per the Long-term Athletic Development plan). Another strikingly similar diminishing intangible—selfish behaviour—was seen by S16 as directly opposed to the enhancing intangible of being a team player: "I think they need to be a team player, like a person that isn't selfish." More on selfish behaviour shortly.

After reviewing this particular diminishing intangible with S5 during the member reflection process, he reinforced the findings by saying, "The lack of enhancing intangibles would decrease the draft status of a player, and I think that's always been the case for anywhere I've been." In this case, S5 was referring to the several different organizations he had previously worked for during his WHL scouting experience. In my own experience with two different WHL organizations, the same can be said about prospects that exhibit deficiencies in any of these enhancing intangibles. Our collective accounts highlight the importance of enhancing intangibles, and how a large deficiency in any one of those enhancers might be detrimental to the draft status of a prospect. Further, this offers strong evidence that teams at higher levels of competition become less interested in an athlete who lacks compete, character, passion, or the ability to be a good teammate.

b) Body Language

"I'm a huge body language guy. When I say body language, I mean I want a kid to look like he's a competitive, engaged human being when I'm watching him. I don't like the eye rolling or the laid-back skating back to the bench. I wanna see guys that are playing whistle to whistle as hard as they can."

— Scout 12

Body language captures the behaviours or interactions that players direct toward themselves or toward other players, coaches, and officials. These are quite often easily seen during competition. Often, bad or poor body language revealed negative behaviours, mannerisms, or interactions that were seen by scouts as an indication of a potential character deficit in players. S3 reaffirmed this notion, and felt that instances of bad body language could indicate larger issues that might exist within a player: "You know, usually bad body language indicates that there's something amiss." Almost exclusively, players' body language was assessed when players were on the ice in game situations. For example, S2 stated:

> I'll try and watch a lot of on-ice stuff. I'll see if they bang their stick after they make a bad play or are they swearing or just constantly, you know, just doing a lot of little things like that. Just body language tells you a lot.

Some scouts felt that the body language of young athletes could easily be detected as described by S9 during his scouting experience:

> You have to look for visual cues, the body language, the interaction, how players react after a missed shot or not getting a pass. And you can see it plain as day, and with kids it's very easy to see sometimes because of their emotional maturity, but that's a red flag.

In a world that is becoming increasingly technologically driven, there has been a large shift toward the use of video scouting. There are several good reasons for scouts to use video, including the potential to cut expenses and the fact that multiple prospects/games can be seen from the comfort of an individual's home in a single day. As previously mentioned, scouting budgets can be a massive expenditure for an organization, so teams might be tempted to gradually utilize video scouts more often. However, in my opinion, this could potentially inhibit the ability to properly evaluate the diminishing intangible of poor body language. Nothing passes the "eye" test quite like seeing a prospect in person, and there are many things that can go unnoticed when watching a video feed instead of being in attendance. This point was underlined by S5, who stated:

I like to hear the noise, I like to hear if kids are talkin'. That's actually a pretty important thing, I think. I feel like for the higher-end players, that's an important part, how they interact with their players or their line mates, with their D partner, with the goalie and while the play is going on, too. I like to hear guys that are yellin' for the puck or recognize something is about to happen and can read that.

c) Selfishness

"Statistics are like bikinis—they show a lot but not everything."

— Lou Pinella

Another undesirable characteristic that was cited by several scouts focused on players that repeatedly displayed selfish behaviours. Increasingly, players at every level of competition are highly motivated by the desire to score goals, accumulate assists, and achieve a degree of offensive production from a statistical perspective. This is not always a necessarily negative attribute, as that is the objective of most team or individual sports—put up more points than the opposition and increase your own team's chances of victory. Many young players might think that higher offensive numbers can increase their individual draft status in the eyes of scouts, coaches, and general managers. However, this behaviour can quickly become problematic if the desire to produce offensive numbers outweighed the team's strategy or objective. As noted by S8, who questioned a player's motivation when a prospect showed more desire to seek offensive points at the expense of the team:

> It's kind of a greedy game in some respects. You want the puck, you wanna score, you wanna be the guy that scores the winning goal. But there's a lot of jealousy and sometimes players don't make smart plays or make plays that are not team oriented.

Junior hockey scouts often took careful note of any behaviour that might indicate a player was putting his own needs to put up points over team objectives. One strategy to gauge selfish behaviour is to closely monitor a player's body language after his own team has scored. An observer can learn from this situation by watching closely (e.g., watching a minor hockey game standing right on the glass, which is a perfect vantage point in most cases), as it can be easy to witness authentic happiness or slight resentment when another player on his/her own line scores. Both reactions (e.g., happiness, or envy) can be very telling regarding a prospect being more team oriented or a player that has selfish tendencies. Scouts also took note of "chiselers"—a term used for players who shout their number to the referee after a goal has been scored in an effort to accumulate more points, even if they did not actually contribute to the eventual goal, and were therefore not deserving of the points. For example, S2 said:

> So, stats aren't everything because again, you know, I think when it comes to goals and assists you can—I've seen in the past where kids are chiseling points and stuff like that. And to me when I see stuff like that, that points to a character flaw.

There was an obvious contempt regarding selfish behaviour that was, at times, bluntly expressed throughout the interview stage, and perhaps why this diminishing intangible required its own subchapter. Perhaps scouts feel that the presence of selfish behaviour can be a destructive force in the creation of a winning culture—sometimes selfishness breeds more selfishness. Another very loose, personal theory is that a good majority of scouts are more than a little old school. In other words, most scouts were once devoutly team players during their own playing days, and as a result believe that hockey is strictly a team game. Again, this is just a personal theory, and a vast overgeneralization, but the following quote by S4 provides a glimpse into the clear disgust for the especially selfish act, labelled chiseling: "Is he a guy that goes and chisels for fucking points? … Is he that guy? Is he that guy that goes to the ref and points to me [i.e. chisels] for the assist?"

Many scout interview quotes suggested that scouts equated selfish behaviour with a lack of character and/or team orientation, and such behaviour could reflect poorly upon the draft status of a prospect. This sentiment was summed up by S7, who said, "If you're a problem child or a selfish person, it doesn't fit into the game of hockey as far as I'm concerned; and that's part of the character that you assess." Interestingly, during his member reflection interview, S16 indicated that some selfish behaviours might actually help a player's performance, but a scout's overall assessment of selfishness was that such behaviour should generally be classified as a diminishing intangible:

> There's been some pretty good players that were selfish. Like Wayne Gretzky [the top points scorer of all time in the NHL], I'm pretty sure was pretty selfish when it came to a lot things [as they related to scoring goals and amassing points during games], but at the end of the day it was that attitude that made him a great player. I guess it depends how you define selfish … a high percentage of the time it would definitely be a diminishing intangible.

Overall, selfish behaviour in hockey appears to be frowned upon within the scouting community, and as such, this seems like a good point to include several additional comments for young hockey players and parents on this subject. Forgive me in advance if this comes across as a rant, but it seems appropriate to express my own personal feelings on the topic of selfishness. Specifically, the obsession with points that seems to be such a priority and focal point for many young players and parents. Yes, points are important, but they are generally only a piece of the overall talent identification puzzle. This is relevant when considering different types of players that any successful team needs. An easy example of a player that could put up zero points and still be highly effective is a defensive first defenceman (D1st)—a player that can match up against the opposition's top players, efficiently kill penalties, and can continually advance the puck out of his own end. In fact, a D1st player could put up zero points during a season and be an extremely valuable member of any team. Further, in my own opinion, every team could use at least two, maybe three, of these types of players to be successful. Another highly valuable role on any team is a two-way or defensive forward that can also match up, shadow, or pester other teams' top players, is good on the draw, willing to kill penalties, etc. The point is, if you are projected as a top-end offensive player, then point production will likely play a factor in the scouting process. However, most teams are fortunate to have four or five forwards, and one or two defencemen that are elite offensive players who are expected to put up big numbers and are labelled genuine threats. Without deviating from a team's standards in terms of playing ability (i.e., skating, skill and hockey sense), this implies that an organization is looking for approximately four defencemen and seven or eight forwards who are fulfilling roles where offensive output is not the main priority.

In junior hockey, the progression from a "role" player to offensive contributor can be more sequential in nature. Meaning, as young players enter the league, they may first have to fill roles where they are not the player that is relied upon for offence, but they may eventually get that opportunity as they develop. Even in this case, players must bide their time and learn other facets of the game to become more well-rounded players. From a distance, the professional landscape in this regard is much different, especially with a salary cap. For one, the progression from a role player to offensive contributor may never happen. A prospect had better be a really good player to take over Ovechkin's or Crosby's role on the power play or get the opportunity to play with McDavid and Draisaitl, or Panarin or Matthews, or any other of the young superstars within the NHL today. If a player is not in that world-class elite level in terms of offensive production, they can still make a great career out of being a bottom six, shutdown player that rarely gets scored on, can kill penalties, and plays ten minutes a game. In fact, from a distance it would appear that the success of an NHL teams often relies on the quality of these type of "cheap" (i.e., NHL minimum salary was $700,000 USD per year) role players, who take pride in providing the reduced number of minutes they are given to accomplish what the team needs from them. Highly skilled offensive prospects often come out of junior or college thinking they are only a top six player, and anything less is beneath them, so they become unwilling to accept a reduced, perhaps more team-oriented role. This even happens at the junior level, and it stunts the progress of many careers.

This is not to suggest that players should abandon skill development and offensive competency, but rather make it less of a be-all and end-all regarding points or playing time. My advice for any young player that wants to continuously advance levels is to take pride in other roles that they are given, and by becoming a more well-rounded, versatile player, a prospect might make themselves more valuable at the next level of play. Further, the identification of players that take pride in and perform these ancillary roles well are, in some cases, harder to find—especially the pride part. Young players who are self-aware enough to know they are not an elite scorer, but can perfect a different role, are often sought-after prospects no matter how many goals or assists they are able to accumulate.

d) Parental Behaviour

"Oftentimes, how the parents behave indicates perhaps how the player is. I think home life is a very significant factor."

— Scout 10

The last diminishing intangible uncovered from the data is one of the more unfortunate realities of youth sport, and a subject that has been well publicized by global media. That is, the many issues associated with undesirable behaviours of players' parents which, by the following accounts, has an undeniable impact on the junior hockey scouting process. As astutely stated by S10:

> Parents have very limited realization that their personal behaviours that they demonstrate in the hockey rink can be very impactful on a scout's perception, because in some ways, when you're drafting a player, you're drafting the family.

This perfectly formulated quote from S10's interview reveals an important impression of parents within the hockey and scouting worlds. Scouts are normally highly observant people by nature, and while they may pick up on many different things on the ice or in the stands, they are likely never going to inform the parent about their potentially harmful behaviour. This is a noteworthy point. Based on my own experience, "problem parents" are usually the last to know that their behaviour, whatever the issue might be, is having a negative impact on their son's evaluation. S16 expanded on that sentiment, noting that the behaviour of parents at the hockey rink can often reflect poorly upon their child:

> I just don't understand when I go to a minor hockey rink, because why as a parent would you be swearing at a probably a 20-something-year-old referee or a maybe a teenage referee and swearing in the stands and yelling at [them]? They're just kids. And if that's your level of emotional control, then that probably is gonna spill off onto your kid.

The list of potential overt behaviours could include a lack of respect shown to other players, parents, and referees, or a general lack of emotional control at games or practices. Unfortunately, the reality of the situation is that it is extremely difficult for a parent to try to contain or mask that habitual and emotional obsession that has built up over years of watching their son play the game they both love. Especially within Canadian youth hockey, which is notorious for producing some of the most bizarre and outlandish behaviour from otherwise normal people. In fact, two of Canada's national newspapers have recently written stories about some of the nutty behaviour of parents across the country. All one needs to do is look at the article titles to get a sense of the content:

- Globe and Mail - *A hockey mom puts herself in the penalty box: What is it about watching your kid play sports that turns ordinary parents into trash-talking, fist-shaking boors.* 11/26/15 - Lars Hegberg
- National Post - *Hockey Parent Confidential: An oral history of sex, bribes and goalie moms.* 3/31/16 - JRiddall

Both articles are a simple google search away and are great reads that contain tales that may shock some readers, but for those who have "been there, done that" (i.e., been involved in hockey as a player, parent, or coach), the article might seem tame—not to mention they could probably add several anecdotes of their own. No matter how a team or individual might describe poor parental behaviour, S12 made it quite clear that his organization would adamantly avoid draft prospects whose parents were deemed problematic:

I'm not drafting a kid with a crazy parent. Like, I've dealt with that too much. I'm not gonna do it. So, if there's a parent up in the stands that's just going crazy, he's negatively affecting his kid's brand.

It would be careless to not mention that some poor parental behaviour is simply a result of parents being unaware of the appropriate behaviour. Often, parents who are not "hockey people" are initially shocked at the drones of scouts at big tournaments or games throughout a season. It can be a daunting experience when they themselves feel like they are under scrutiny, or do not realize that they themselves are being evaluated. Further, the behaviour does not always have to be exhibited overtly. Individuals unfamiliar with certain nuances of the game could likely benefit from the often-used phrase, "the hockey world is a small one." Believe me, it is true, and stories travel fast. During his interview, S13 provided his account of how chatty scouts can be: "I'll have to say scouts like to talk too, they hear something negative behind the scenes. Sooner or later, everybody's gonna know it or somebody's gonna know it, and it's gonna spread." That said, my advice for new parents in any sport is: get excited, be involved in a positive, supportive way, but most importantly, just enjoy the experience, because it goes by quickly.

Other instances of poor parental behaviour might happen behind the scenes, and in my own estimation, can be more destructive than getting a little too amped up during your child's game. Every season, there seems to be more stories about a parent, or group of parents, who try to manipulate coaching decisions regarding who their sons play with, or the power play unit, or any other number of issues that parents overanalyze relating to their son's performance. In my opinion, these shady, manipulative tactics so your son can enhance his numbers or status is truly the epitome of a "crazy" parent. When this behaviour surfaces, us crusty old scouts always try to compare that kind of behaviour with a real-life analogy. For example, one of us might say, "Imagine 15 years after [insert prospect] has finished playing, and the dad tries to reach out to his son's boss to get him a promotion or raise." It is ludicrous behaviour to even imagine, and sets such an enormously bad precedence for youth, but it happens—a lot.

Many readers could debate the research results and eventual labelling of parental behaviour as a diminishing intangible that works against a young player, because it is out of said prospect's control. Certainly, a valid argument, and an extremely unfair predicament for a young player whose parents may want him to become a professional more than he himself might aspire to be. Despite the validity of this argument, the topic was so prevalent that it became unavoidable, so there was really no way to avoid reporting this impact in the results. Whether it can be labelled as an intangible could be a fruitful avenue for future research. However, at the very minimum, perhaps if parents knew that their overt or manipulative actions were hurting their son's chances of being evaluated properly, then maybe this knowledge could help. That would be personally gratifying.

In the end, the overall impact that negative or inappropriate parental behaviours had upon the evaluative process of junior hockey scouts was summed up by S7 during his member reflection interview: "When you see poor parental behaviour, that probably rubs you the wrong way. And, consciously or not, you tend to walk away from the kid, or factor it in [as a diminishing intangible], rightly or wrongly."

Throughout this exploration of intangibles, there have been several times where the content expert (CE) provided a fresh perspective on several of the themes generated in this junior hockey study. Depending on the prospect, the CE suggested that his team might consider choosing the talent and skill of a world-class prospect regardless of any glaring diminishing intangibles the player might have displayed. However, that did not mean the CE completely dismissed diminishing intangibles, and undoubtedly, he also noted that some of these negative characteristics could create a cause for concern when he said, "Sometimes it's parents, sometimes it's work ethic, sometimes their 'give a fuck meter' is so low." In fact, the CE referred to his team creating a "no draft" list, which was assigned to players that possessed all of the technical, tactical, and physical abilities of a first-round draft selection, but whose diminishing intangibles were too significant for the team to overlook. This provides further evidence that diminishing intangibles can be a factor in the evaluation of players at both the junior and professional level. Whether the issue was undesirable parental behaviours, being a selfish player, or displaying bad body language, diminishing intangibles can negatively impact the draft status of players and lead to the assignment of what many scouts referred to as red flags. These red flags, described in more detail in the next chapter, are carefully considered during the final evaluation phase of the scouting process prior to an upcoming WHL draft as teams settled on "The List."

Chapter 8
"The List"

THE FINAL STAGE OF THE SCOUTING PROCESS WAS THE CRE-
ation of a coveted document known as "The List." Twelve of the 16
junior scouts mentioned The List during their interviews, making note of the
role it played in determining a player's draft status (i.e., where a player would
be ranked), or whether a player would be drafted at all. When discussing
this document during interviews, scouts normally made mention that both
enhancing and diminishing intangibles played a role in moving players up
or down a team's respective list. For example, S1 said, "There are guys that I
think either eliminate themselves from a certain spot in the draft, or guys that
will move up slightly because of that [intangible]." Regarding diminishing
intangibles, S11 described how they could potentially drop a player down his
organization's list:

> There's sometimes when he could be a first-round pick,
> but he's dropped to seventh or eighth round because of
> his character, because of the way he acted, the way he
> played, the way he comes across, maybe what the coaches
> said about him, or maybe his parents, they play a vital role
> in the position too.

In both quotes, S1 and S11 appear to imply that diminishing intangibles have
a stronger downward effect on the status of a prospect on their team's respective
list. Further, several scouts referenced a potential imbalance between the stronger
impact diminishing intangibles had on the evaluation of a prospect when making
final decisions about the draft status of a player. For example, S3 said:

> There's a lot of those players that if I liked what they do
> in terms of how they play the game in terms of their skill
> characteristics, and I don't like some of the things that
> they do in terms of their intangibles, then that player will
> not end up on my list.

That same sentiment was reinforced by S4 when he stated, "I think a guy with poor intangibles, you just don't draft at all, they don't even go in your draft list." In yet another example, S12 underlined the negative impact of diminishing intangibles saying:

> Well, they're definitely significant. I would say that they become more significant if they're negative intangibles. So, if I'm hearing that a kid is, you know, got bad character or not a team guy, those are gonna sink a kid more than someone that I don't hear positive reviews about.

The above collection of quotes appears to suggest that diminishing intangibles may indeed have a stronger impact on the evaluation of a player than enhancing intangibles. While it would require another research project to confirm this suggestion, maybe young hockey players are just expected to work hard, be passionate about the game, be a strong team player, and a good person. In other words, hockey players and athletes are simply expected to embody all enhancing intangibles. If this is the expectation, then young athletes might benefit from age-appropriate educational programs that are designed to help them develop these enhancing attributes.

An integral part of creating The List includes grouping and comparing players that are deemed deserving of being draft worthy based on playing ability and investigative information compiled throughout the season. During this preparation and subsequent comparison process, scouts taking part in the research described how their respective organizations' scouting staffs would discuss any red flags that raised concerns about the suitability or draft status of a player:

> It's a discussion, you know; here's a very good player and we've got a decision to make on three or four players. And a negative point comes out on this player. If we can prove the negativity of that point, we might not decide on that player and pick somebody that doesn't have that trait. (S13)

The term "red flag" can be used in sports to describe a player, prospect, or trade option that might come with undesirable characteristics, or diminishing intangibles, that could potentially create a negative influence within an organization. The assignment of red flags to a player within our junior hockey research was founded upon the identification of a diminishing intangible, or the lack of apparent enhancing intangibles. The following quote by S7 illustrates how a lack of passion or compete can be a red flag:

> I can think back over the last several years where there's a guy who is really skilled and you know that they're probably going to put up X amount of points, but I don't see the passion or drive from them. To me that's a big red flag, and that's something I wouldn't want personally in our organization.

It is extremely important to note that the assignment of red flags and the resulting decision about a player is an ongoing, objective result in most cases. That said, when scouts did uncover potential red flags about a prospect, they would initially grant a player with the benefit of the doubt. In other words, junior hockey scouts were cognizant that any revelation about a 14-year-old prospect would require further investigation. This was noted by S12, who noted, "it's not something, it's not a one strike and you're done, but if I look and dig in all different levels and find the same thing about a kid again—not a good teammate, not competitive, out for himself—[we are not going to draft him]." Early teenage years can be fragile at the best of times, and an array of factors can potentially affect kids on a daily basis, including academic pressure, social stressors, and parental expectations—not to mention the athletic demands placed upon young players. Therefore, it would be irresponsible for any junior scout to automatically write off a young athlete after witnessing or hearing something less than desirable. However, in many cases, the axiom "where there is smoke there is fire" applies. If more red flags were subsequently revealed during a team's investigative efforts, then this normally would have a cumulative negative impact upon a player's draft status. In fact, some teams routinely created a red flag list for certain players that they would intentionally avoid drafting, as outlined by S12: "We have a red flag list that if there's something real big and that's going to drastically affect their draft status, they get put on the red flag list." Furthermore, if multiple red flags about a highly talented prospect are raised, then an organization might decide to drop or push the prospect down their list to a spot where they think he will likely be selected before they would make that consideration. This was described further by S12:

> And we always talk about that at draft day too, that we'll place a kid somewhere where we can't get him because someone will take him way before we will. That's just because we don't really want him. And we call it our gut feeling too. [If] your gut feeling's not good on a kid, get him down the list.

It may sound harsh, but in my own scouting experience, this strategy effectively works like a stop order in stock trading. Stop limit orders are used to buy or sell a security when its price moves past a specific point, ensuring a higher probability of achieving a predetermined entry or exit price, thereby limiting the investor's loss, or locks in a profit. The difference, of course, is that in this case a team is limiting the risk of selecting a physically, technically, or tactically talented player with red flags by not selecting that prospect until after he has dropped to a certain round. Depending on the red flag attached to the prospect, this might be a fair approach in limiting the risk associated with a talented prospect with questionable intangibles.

That said, a team should have a definitive backup plan in this scenario. More specifically, a team will need to consider a firm answer to the question: If player X is available in round Z, then what? The answer will vary from team to team, but if an organization is adamant about maintaining or developing a strong culture, then the later rounds might be the best place in the draft to select players with as many enhancing intangibles as possible. Again, during my own experience with these types of picks, the risk has been properly factored into the equation. In other words, they can be a waste of a pick; the better option is to take a less skilled player with exceptional enhancing intangibles.

The continuous balancing, re-balancing, and final placement of players on an organization's list are the decisions the scouting staff will deliberate upon, right up until the day of the draft. During his member reflection interview, S5 described how his organization's evaluation of diminishing intangibles versus desirable physical/technical attributes can impact the final decisions about draft prospects:

> I know in instances in the past with teams I worked for, there's been guys we've taken right off our list and it had nothing to do with his skill, like he could be one of the more skilled guys even in the draft, but there's just too many of those other issues, other red flags, you know, negative intangibles that just outweigh the positives.

Whether a scouting staff was considering the final order of players on their respective lists preparing for the draft, or making a quick audible at the table, intangibles often acted as a tiebreaker when the final decision was ultimately made. This was articulated by S1:

> You consider two guys that are very similar, like with their point output, or their skillset, or whatever, but the one guy with the better intangibles is always going to be the guy that we pick at that one point. The intangibles always win out if guys are close.

Scouting staffs face difficult decisions every draft, and as the rounds evolve, they must continuously decide between highly comparable (e.g., playing ability) players on their respective lists. These difficulties create the tie-breaking decisions whereby scouts rely on intangibles to help them navigate through those decisions. Further, S10 described how intangibles are also in some ways connected to the success of the player within the organization:

> You want to make sure that you're confident that you're going to select a draft player that has optimal opportunity for positive impact in your organization. So, when you're watching players, the on-ice differences might be minimal as far as their ability to get from A to B quickly, to win puck battles, to be strong on possession. That's where the tiebreakers, if you will, the intangibles, become critically important.

Scouts also felt that using intangibles to determine the best tie-breaking decisions became particularly important during the middle to late rounds, where most lists contained players with very similar physical ability and skill. For example, S5 stated:

> When you're in that draft and you're getting into the middle rounds and you're looking at a lot of kids that are very similar ... and they possess pretty much identical skill and those common characteristics that we've talked about [i.e., obvious playing ability], I think if you like one kid's leadership skills more than the other, that's probably the guy you're going with.

Another similar opinion was shared by S10, who felt that the most physically/technically talented players were likely selected after the first two rounds of a draft, at which point his staff began looking for players that best fit the organization's needs:

> After the first two rounds, the best players are gone. So, who's the best player, defenseman or forward? You could say, well this guy's the best player because he scores more points or he might be the best player in the position, but who's the best player for our organization?

Again, for young players and parents, it is crucial to understand that the "best players" only refer to that specific moment in time. Any junior hockey draft will only provide a snapshot of a young player's development, especially in the WHL where the teams are selecting a year earlier than the OHL or QMJHL. Can this glimpse provide a solid preview of the future potential of a player? Absolutely, but regardless of the age or format, players that are eligible for any junior hockey draft will still be experiencing different growth and maturity patterns. In other words, when it comes to maturity—whether it be physical, emotional, or psychological—some players will be ahead and others might be behind. The main point regarding this disparity in maturity of junior hockey prospects is this: the best prospects at the bantam age (U15) may not always be the best prospects over the long term. There are plenty of NHL players who were passed over in the WHL draft, including Jarome Iginla, Jamie Benn, Shea Weber, Jake Bean, and Rick Rypien to name a few. Candidly, the disparity of player maturity, or Relative Age Effect (RAE) was not covered within our U of A research. However, in the time that has passed since, it seems reasonable to consider whether enhancing and diminishing intangibles have more of an impact at the junior hockey level because of these varied maturity levels. During my own scouting experience, there have been plenty of instances where players who are physically mature have typically been the best players prior to their bantam draft year. However, because these "early maturers" were always bigger, stronger, and faster than their peers and hence better, they often develop bad habits. Some examples of these bad habits might include poor skating technique or sloppy tactical habits (e.g., they become the one man show and think that they can play that way straight into the NHL), and as a result they can develop poor intangibles as well. On the flip side, the player that matures later, and the individual who continually works for everything he gets, will often excel when their physical development starts to catch up. An excellent, recent example would be Cale Makar of the Colorado Avalanche - an eighth round WHL pick (he did choose to play Junior A for the Brooks Bandits) and a fourth overall NHL pick. The question of maturity regarding intangibles is only food for thought at this time, but also another potential avenue for longitudinal research.

Based on the information and examples provided in this chapter, it appears diminishing intangibles have a stronger and more harmful impact on the evaluation of a junior hockey prospect. Further, junior hockey scouts rely on the evaluation of prospect intangibles to decide a tiebreaker, which could suggest they are choosing players who might be a better fit for the organization. In other words, if scouts are relying on intangibles to make a final decision about a group of players with similar playing ability, then most organizations would rather select a prospect with enhancing intangibles than an individual that has been flagged with diminishing intangibles. Perhaps most importantly, young athletes that continue to develop the enhancing intangibles of hard work, focusing on team play, passion for the game, and becoming a good person should ultimately thrive in any long-term endeavour they pursue (e.g., education, community service, employment). There are plenty of individuals within sport research, specifically the Positive Youth Development movement, that would argue this is the systemic purpose and benefit of youth sport on a global scale (Holt et al., 2017 & Lerner et al., 2011).

Chapter 9

Culture

"I think just there's a lot of times that you're watching players throughout a year and you see things that give you concern. If it's something that you feel is an issue for the way that you have created a culture within your group, then certainly you have to address that. And that means not taking that player or staying away from it, you know you never want to start with a toxic environment—you want to have your environment set and you want it to be the way you've instilled in your player [as] the right way to do things."

— Scout 3

THROUGHOUT THE ANALYSIS PROCESS, A BIG PICTURE THEME began to emerge regarding the potential influence organizational culture has on a scout's perception of intangibles. For example, S8 described how his team's scouting staff all shared a similar perception of the enhancing or diminishing intangible characteristics:

> I think all teams do a very good job of evaluating players. I don't think there's a lot of secrets, but I think there is an advantage. Some teams have more success than others I think, by what they perceive to be intangibles.

Thematic analysis also suggested that junior hockey scouts used the available information from their existing organizational culture, team identity, and team dynamics as being akin to a "map" of intangibles. Some scouts referred to this map when trying to weigh, measure, and evaluate different intangibles of draft-eligible players during the evaluation process. During his member reflection interview, S1 provided a great example of this sentiment when he said, "the culture of a club kind of dictates where you go with those things [i.e., intangibles] and how much emphasis you put on them, and you know, which ones you find most important." Junior hockey scouts also seemed to use this cultural map as a guide to predict how incoming players might fit into or disrupt the established organizational culture and social dynamic of the team. For example, S3 made the following assertion regarding the protection of his team's culture: "If there's things [i.e., attributes] on that player that I don't foresee as being positive or something that would skew our team or change the environment that we have within our organization, then I will avoid that player at all costs." This sentiment was further expanded upon by S9 when he stated, "that's why I think it's important [for all members of the scouting staff] to identify what you want your team to look like, and does this player fit into that group." These interview excerpts provide key testimony regarding the apparent connection between organizational culture and how members of a respective scouting staff consider, define, and eventually evaluate enhancing or diminishing intangibles.

In several cases, scouts referenced occasions where they may have strayed from the course of their figurative intangible map and later regretted their detour. For example, one scout recounted an occasion where his team had learned the hard way when they ignored the criticality of intangibles and instead chose the best player in terms of physical playing ability. The following narrative provides the backdrop of a time when S12 and his team knowingly overlooked several diminishing intangibles of a highly talented/ skilled player:

> This kid's got unbelievable skill and skating, you know. He leaves a little bit to be desired over here [i.e., character flaws], but I think that once we get him into our organization, once we get him around our good people and once we get him into, you know, doing things our way, he'll straighten that part out, but he will flourish with the other parts. *We found that it doesn't really work that way* [emphasis added].

During his member reflection interview, S10 further expanded upon the hazards of drafting players who could potentially disrupt the current team culture: "With respect to your culture, it doesn't take much more than one or two mistakes if you will—by bringing in the wrong people—and suddenly your culture is at risk." Combined, these participant comments suggest that despite the exceptional playing abilities of a junior hockey prospect, a potential player can have a detrimental impact on an established organizational culture if glaring diminishing intangibles are overlooked—assuming the organizational culture is a good one.

Thus far, the presentation of information collected during junior hockey scout interviews seemingly implies the notion of organizational culture having an influence on the prevailing intangibles that scouts consider during the evaluation of bantam age (U15) players. However, readers might wonder if this apparent intersection between culture and intangibles is relevant at the professional level. Again, my experience at the professional level stands at zero, so it would be impossible, and irresponsible, for me to comment on how these findings might translate to the professional level. That said, it does not take long to find specific cases that help reinforce the suggestion that culture might be a consideration for evaluating the intangibles of players at the professional level.

For example, during the writing process of this book, a story was released regarding a player that was discussed in Chapter 1—Nail Yakupov—who ended up being the first overall selection by the Edmonton Oilers in the 2012 NHL entry draft. During a 2020 interview, Brian Burke, the general manager of the Toronto Maple Leafs in 2012, candidly revealed he and his scouting staff's perception of Yakupov after they had interviewed him prior to the 2012 draft. When Burke was asked about his opinion of Yakupov leading up to the 2012 NHL draft, he bluntly declared, "We weren't going to take him. His draft interview was the worst interview I've ever had in my life. Terrible; he was defiant, obnoxious, and sullen" (Wegman, 2020).

Wow! Normally, the public would never hear an NHL executive be so blunt about a player or situation in that manner, but Mr. Burke made these comments as a member of the media (SportsNet). This was a strong statement, especially years after the fact, but what is significant in this case is that the Leafs' impression of Yakupov proved to be somewhat accurate. Further, Toronto had the fifth overall selection that same year, so they could have potentially been considering Yakupov if he had dropped a few spots, or if the Leafs had chosen to trade up in the draft for a higher selection—a tactic Burke had employed when he successfully orchestrated a trade that would land Daniel and Henrik Sedin with the second and third overall picks during the 1999 NHL entry draft as general manager of the Vancouver Canucks. However, during the 2012 NHL draft, Burke and the Leafs stood pat and chose one of the better, arguably best, prospects available in 2012—defence-man Morgan Rielly from the Moose Jaw Warriors of the WHL. Rielly, an assistant captain with Toronto since 2016, has played 500 plus games and collected 270 points during his first seven seasons in the NHL. Retrospectively, Rielly was a great selection at number five. Yakupov. Not so much.

The content expert (CE) also shared an additional explanation as to why teams may want to avoid players that exhibit questionable intangibles based on the broader organizational culture. The CE described how other members, (e.g., coaching staff, skill development/strength and conditioning personnel, executive staff, etc.), outside the scouting staff, are the individuals most impacted by the type of individuals the team drafts and eventually brings into the organization. In fact, our CE made certain that his staff take the time to consider how a potential prospect that had been assigned red flags might relate with different people from within the broader organization. By having his staff consider that potential impact, the eventual discussion could influence where a prospect was placed on their final list as they collectively envisioned how the player might, or might not, fit in with the ancillary members of the organization:

> Sometimes you've got to determine the separation between the organization and the scouts. Like, the scouts want the best player, but then once the scouts pick 'em, they're done with them, and then the organization is stuck with 'em!

This is a great recommendation for members of a scouting staff to consider: be aware of the implications your recommendations might make on the organizational culture when collecting information regarding the intangibles of potential draft or trade prospects. This concept can be easy to forget for members of a scouting staff, as they normally attend training camp and then set off in their own direction to evaluate prospects available in the next talent pool. Much of the time, members of the scouting staff are on the road, away from the team, and may not give much consideration to the day-to-day of players after camp. While this might sound trivial, it speaks to the larger picture and importance of organizational culture. A strong culture should create an environment where each person is pulling the same chain, in the same direction, and understand that every decision they make could affect someone else within the organization. A common misconception about culture in sport is that it only applies to the players. Of course, players are a crucial part of organizational culture in sport, but equally or more important is the leadership that is tasked with creating the foundation of what an organization does, why it does the things it does, and how it goes about doing those things (ICSA, 2018). The cultural direction and decisions of leadership should eventually trickle down to members of the staff at all levels, then onto the players (ICSA, 2018). The players in a specific organization are normally the stakeholders that are expected to uphold the values, morals, and tradition of the culture in question. The intersections between culture, talent identification, and selection will be further explored in Chapter 12 during Final Thoughts.

Review - Cultural Connections

During the junior hockey exploration of intangibles and talent identification, 11 scouts referred to the existing culture or social climate of their respective organizations. More specifically, the intangible characteristics that were most closely considered by scouts appear to have been influenced by the culture or social dynamics that either exist or are sought within their respective organizations. Within the corporate or small business field there are intriguing parallels between talent identification decisions made in sport with the hiring and selection practices of successful organizations. In fact, organizational psychology literature has recognized that personnel selection is often viewed as "a means to further organizational strategic objectives" ((Schmitt, Cortana, Ingerick, & Wiechmann, 2003). In junior hockey terms this means that most, if not all, WHL teams want to put a winning product on the ice—and these strategic objectives are best accomplished when future members of the organization (i.e., players) have the competencies or skills to successfully fulfill the job requirements (i.e., to be able to compete in the WHL). This obviously translates into both business organizations and sport teams needing to build teams with individuals that have the necessary abilities or talent to help them succeed. In other words, a business would not succeed by hiring a botanist to perform engineering duties just as a hockey team will not win many games if they are selecting players that lack adequate playing capabilities. Additionally, organizational psychology literature also suggests that matching the values, beliefs, and attitudes of individuals recruited with those held by the organization can help businesses reach their strategic objectives (Garcia-Izquierdo, Vilela, & Moscoso, 2015). Successful organizations try to find or select people with "internal values, norm beliefs, underlying assumptions, attitudes, and behaviours" that are upheld within the business (Garcia-Izquierdo et al., 2015). Thus, the presence of a clear organizational culture can be used to guide the types of people who are hired/selected, or not hired/selected, by specific organizations. This becomes significant when comparing the results from our junior hockey study and actual businesses wanting to hire not only qualified, but also like-minded individuals. This suggests that organizational culture or team climate, which can include behavioural, attitudinal, and interpersonal standards expected of athletes by the organization, can play an important role in determining the intangible characteristics that are considered by scouts during the evaluation period of potential draft prospects.

Exploring intersections that might exist between the selection decisions made in sport and business uncovers some excellent examples. Researching culturally driven organizations reveals cases of overlapping selection decisions that can be mutually beneficial for both sport and business domains, whereby they can learn from one another's methods. One prevalent example is the 2013 book *Legacy*, by James Kerr, subtitled *What the All Blacks can teach us about the business of life*. In my humble opinion, this book is an absolute masterpiece and must read for any person that is interested in the literal definition of a successful organizational culture. The book has become a blueprint on how to build, develop, and maintain a winning culture within high performing teams in sport or business. In the book, Kerr speaks at length about the role team culture and values play in the selection of players who earn the opportunity to compete for the All Blacks—New Zealand's world-renowned men's rugby team. Kerr recounts instances of players who had the physical, technical, and tactical abilities to compete at the highest levels of international rugby, but were not selected because their behaviours and/or attitudes simply did not fit with the established cultural expectations and standards of the team. For example, one of the team's policies that was instituted to help govern players and staff alike was coined "no dickheads." The no dickheads policy applied to the day-to-day activities of the team, but also had an impact on the selection of athletes. As noted by Kerr, "The All Blacks place ... emphasis on their fundamental and foundational [team] values, going so far as to select on character over talent" (p. 18). Sound familiar? Personally speaking, one of the most fascinating features of the All Blacks' rigorous adherence to cultural values is when you take the time to think about the implications in a familiar context. More specifically, the silver fern worn on the chests of

New Zealand's finest rugby players is analogous to the maple leaf stitched on the front of Canadian hockey jerseys. Think about that for a moment. Based on Kerr's quote regarding the selection of players with character over talent, and how that might work with Hockey Canada. Imagine a Canadian hockey team not selecting a player like Connor McDavid because he happened to be a "dickhead." Of course, this is a completely hypothetical situation to convey the underlying cultural message in the case of the All Blacks. From the little I do know about Connor McDavid, he is reported to be an exceptional person, but this example illustrates the magnitude and importance of the cultural values that are upheld with the All Blacks culture. These now engrained cultural values seem to have worked, and undoubtedly have played a crucial role in the All Blacks' historical success as the most winningest sports team over the last century. And yes, you read that correctly—the highest winning percentage of any sports team during the last one hundred years.

Within academic research there are plenty of examples that portray the degree in which team culture or team climate are considered by selectors/ coaches in the evaluation process of athletes. During a study examining NCAA coaches' perceptions of the strategies by which team culture can be developed, or in this case protected, a Division 1 volleyball head coach provided the following brusque statement about a potential top recruit:

> There's a guy who is going to be one of the top five recruits in the [sic] America next year. I'm not even going to call him. He's an asshole. I saw him a couple of weeks ago yelling at his coach, and I thought I'm not bringing that in. And I don't care how good he is. I know there are other schools that are desperate for him. He may be great. He may be a turnaround kind of player for them, but I'm not willing to sacrifice what kind of environment we have here (Schroeder, 2010).

This might seem exceedingly forceful, but it also highlights the protective ferocity of some organizations regarding the culture they have developed and steadfastly want to sustain. In this example, the coach makes it overwhelmingly clear that the collective environment of the team far outweighs the talent of any single prospect, regardless of how talented or coveted that player might be. Further, this NCAA coach's declaration matches the sentiment provided by S10 in our own research when he claimed, "It doesn't take much more than one or two mistakes if you will—by bringing in the wrong people—that suddenly your culture is at risk." Apologies to readers for using this quote on three separate occasions, but it is such a powerful statement, and one that I steadfastly agree with should an organization want to sustain or create a healthy culture.

This combined evidence suggests that if an organization wants to consistently select/draft/recruit the right prospects, then individual scouts should understand the existing, or desired, culture and team climate within their respective organizations. This approach aligns with Schroeder's (2010) research results indicating head coaches of successful NCAA Division 1 programs had developed "very specific recruiting profiles and scouting techniques ... to recruit players who embodied the team values." These team values were used to evaluate:

- the way recruits would interact with coaches and teammates on an interpersonal level;
- the way recruits would add to the tactical performance-based needs of the team; and
- the way recruits would demonstrate a commitment to the behavioural expectations of the team as they related to work ethic, discipline, attitude, and effort.

This may require an initial exertion of effort by executive management and senior members of the club, but organizations employing a scouting staff could benefit from reviewing, updating, and periodically relaying the team values and beliefs to said members. By providing an organizational cultural mission statement, members of a scouting staff could potentially and regularly find the best players in terms of physical ability, but also prospects with intangibles that match the cultural values, beliefs, and attitudes of the entire organization.

Chapter 10

Intangible Review & Application

WHILE IT MAY SOUND SELF-RIGHTEOUS, THE GOAL FOR THIS book is to try to make a small impact on the game of hockey, and youth sport in general. More specifically, I sincerely hope that the contents of both the research and this book might contain valuable information for young players who are hoping to be drafted into the WHL or any other junior hockey league. On a grander scale, the goal was to provide a few key takeaways that could benefit any young athlete whose hope it is to one day play at a higher level of competition, regardless of the sport. There is no denying the fact that physical, technical, and tactical skill will always form the primary basis of evaluation in the eyes of most evaluators, but this book was designed to shed light on the importance of something deeper than just athletic prowess—the value of a player's character (i.e., the person behind the player) in the evaluation process. As such, I believe that young athletes can benefit from educational programs that focus on not only physical development, but also character development. During my graduate studies, it gradually and increasingly became clear that the genuine benefit of children participating in sport was founded in the principles of positive youth development (PYD). Quoting directly from the Lions Quest Canada—The Centre for Positive Youth Development website, "PYD is an approach to intentionally structuring opportunities, supports and services for youth so that young people develop the skills they need to thrive and transition smoothly into adulthood. Positive Youth Development deliberately seeks to increase the number of protective factors surrounding a young person that can ultimately translate into more positive social behaviours and reduced negative risk-taking behaviours." Nearly every young athlete will dream of the glamour and fame of professional sport, but the realistic calculation equates to only a small percentage of youngsters being fortunate enough to reach the top level of any given sport. I know this cold fact often irks young players, and some parents, but it also makes the case for PYD that much stronger. Combining

PYD goals with potential learnings available from the promotion of enhancing intangibles and avoidance of diminishing intangibles could provide value for young athletes in two ways:

1. Learning how and why developing character and other intangibles can improve their draft status in the eyes of the scouting community.

2. The genuine realization that falling short of the professional ranks is not failure, because the journey of sport can lead individuals into other positions where they can make positive contributions to society at large (Holt et al., 2017).

I get it. In our modern world, these outcomes are far from glitzy, but they highlight the fundamental objective of why humans created and play sports—for the competition, comradery, and overall value of physical fitness. There is no question about the challenge in conveying this message to young athletes and them truly appreciating the intentions, but even if they understand it later in life, it might be worth promoting further.

A good start would be if parents were able to grasp these same realizations, because they are just as important, if not more, in comprehending the value of these long-term lessons. If parents truly bought in to these long-term benefits of sport, then it might reduce some of the angst, manipulation, and competition between parents that starts well before the child has any clue why mom, dad, or both are acting in a certain manner. That said, this book should also have provided useful information and several practical implications for parents of young athletes who are seeking to compete at higher levels of competition. Not only for the overt behaviour of parents at their children's hockey games, but also for those operating behind the scenes and in the shadows. I sincerely hope that by reading this book it became clear that many scouts pay attention to the behaviours of parents at hockey games, where instances of unruly, disruptive, or manipulative behaviour could undermine the draft status of their child. Further, scouts may witness or hear many things that make them cringe on the inside, but they maintain a perfect poker face during the entire evaluation process. Unfortunately, some parents are the last to know.

A close friend of mine who was once a very good hockey player—a 1994 NHL draft pick—and whose daughter has never participated in hockey, made the best point I have heard about parents in the game. He made the point that parenting in hockey is somewhat of a zero-sum game. What he meant was that parents start at zero and can never add points to their figurative score; they can only lose points. That same point of view came across in the results of our research. Even when given the opportunity, no scouts alluded to good parenting behaviour that might enhance the draft status of a player, but nearly 70% of scouts within the study specifically mentioned bad parenting behaviour that could diminish the draft status of a player. As noted earlier, a recent study on the concept of "exemplary parenting" in youth sport (Pynn, Dunn, & Holt, 2019) emphasised the importance that both coaches and parents placed upon parents' ability to control their emotions and corresponding behaviours before, during, and after competitions. Often, emotional control is linked to emotional intelligence (Salovey & Mayer, 1990), which indicates applied educational interventions could be used to help parents attune or increase their own emotional intelligence (Ciarrochi & Mayer, 2007). Further, I think that many parents would be more than happy to take part in an educational program that was not punitively designed. Instead, parents could learn they might be able to help their young hockey player's efforts in being drafted or recruited to play at a higher level of competition. Again, this is part of the value of providing information for those parents who would like to know the kind of messages they should be reinforcing at home, the car ride to and from, or around the rink. At the end of the day, I would pose one serious question to any parent who has a young athlete involved in sport: If you are truly interested in the development of your child, is there anything wrong with helping them develop a strong work ethic, encourage being a good teammate, developing leadership skills, following their passion and just being a good person? If the answer is no, not at all, then reinforcing enhancing intangibles and avoiding diminishing intangibles might create a great long-term foundation for the overall development of your child as an athlete, but most important of all, as a person.

Finally, this book may offer practical value for individuals working in the talent-identification industry, and particularly those in the junior hockey scouting ranks. Specifically, individuals who are starting their scouting career might be well advised that talent identification in youth sport goes beyond what a person might see on the ice, field, pitch, court, diamond, etc. In other words, simply having the knowledge to assess the performance-based skills or the accurate assessment of players' physical, technical, and tactical abilities of a hockey player (or soccer player, football player, baseball player, basketball player, etc.), while valuable, may not be entirely sufficient when trying to make a fully informed decision about the draft or recruitment suitability of a prospect. It is therefore recommended that scouts, selectors, and evaluators learn about the harder to measure attributes of the person beyond the player when making decisions about which players to select, or not select, in the evaluation process. Although performance-based analytics (e.g., statistical summaries of shooting percentage, shots toward goal, possession rates, etc.) continue to play a large role within sport and talent identification (Gerrard, 2017; Vollman, 2016), these statistics do not provide the organization any information about the person, their values, or the interpersonal skills of the prospect. As highlighted throughout the entirety of this book, the person and the values they possess are important matters for an organization to consider before deciding to draft, recruit, or sign a prospect. Previous research has shown that interpersonal or relationship conflicts within sport teams can have an extremely debilitating impact upon team members (Holt, Knight, & Zukiwski, 2012), which can also undermine overall team performance (De Dreu & Weingart, 2003). However, it is exciting to think about some of the possibilities that could result from these technological innovations. By combining the increasing technological advancement of player tracking systems used for analytic purposes, it is not impossible to think that these systems could also play a role in tracking certain behavioural tendencies identified in this study that might reveal information about certain intangible player characteristics valued by scouts. For example, considering the overall compete level of a prospect is a highly valued attribute for scouts in the evaluation process. Perhaps someone far smarter than myself could develop a tracking system designed to generate statistics around skating speed or the number of all out sprints a player makes throughout a game. By adding different functions, such as the score or time remaining in a game, an organization might be able to render useful scouting statistics regarding the overall compete level of a player over the course of an entire season. This type of analytical statistic could one day be used to supplement the scouts' observational assessments of this intangible player characteristic. As shown throughout the book, the TiD process is continually evolving and looking for ways to further improve or refine the process.

Enhancing Intangibles Review

The overarching purpose of this book was to explore, identify, and provide information about intangible player characteristics that junior hockey scouts consider when determining the draft-suitability of minor hockey players. More specifically, the book, based on graduate level research, was driven by three primary questions: (1) What are the intangible player characteristics that junior hockey scouts consider when evaluating draft-eligible prospects? (2) Why are these intangible player characteristics deemed important in the evaluation process? and (3) How do junior hockey scouts gather and use intangible player characteristics in making their final decisions about the draft suitability of draft-eligible players?

However, before a scout even thinks about a player's intangibles, they first need to attend to the first step in the talent identification process: find the most talented players in terms of physical, technical, and tactical abilities. As a scout, you must be able to identify players with the ability and skill to contribute at the next level of play. Within junior hockey, scouts overwhelmingly identified that an ability to skate was the most important physical characteristic for potential junior hockey players. In fact, skating is a critical skill for young hockey players to continually improve upon and advance within the game. In general, there seems to be a level of agreement about the evaluation of other physical, technical, and tactical skills such as puck skill, shot, goal-scoring ability, playmaking ability, and hockey sense. While ratings from team to team might differ slightly, scouts within this research project felt that the evaluation of playing ability was a straightforward, "objective" task whereby experienced scouts would generally agree on assigned ranks or grades of players according to these physical attributes. As S5 said, "I think most of the guys that are involved in our league would have a pretty good idea at that point, assessing those general [physical] characteristics, after seeing them four or five times." Only after scouts had identified the prospects they wanted to monitor over a season did they turn their collective attention to the less obvious, or harder to grade (i.e., intangible), characteristics. Scouts felt that these intangibles provided insight into the person behind the player and could help determine whether the athlete would be a good fit for a scout's team/organization.

As scouts identified players with sufficient physical skills, they then sought more information about the person beyond the player. The results from the U of A research revealed that the collection of information about players was compared to an ongoing investigation of draft prospects. In other words, evaluations were based upon multiple observations from multiple people within the organization over a prolonged period. These efforts were made to ensure that the most informed decisions could be made by scouts and their respective organizations regarding the draft status of prospects (cf. Neely et al., 2016). For the most part, information about intangible characteristics of prospects began with on-ice observations of players. Again, these on-ice viewings provided scouts an opportunity to gauge whether prospects met the criteria set out by an organization in terms of "tangible" playing ability. Once the physical, or tangible, ability of prospects had been assessed, scouts then shifted their attention toward intangibles, using several different sources of information including questionnaires, social media, formal or informal interviews with players, parents, coaches, managers, and even trainers. Each respective scouting staff will employ a different combination of information sources to provide additional insight into the intangible characteristics of players. However, it is important to acknowledge that decisions are rarely, if ever, based upon any single source of information (e.g., social media). Regardless of how scouts gathered information about draft-eligible prospects, there is clearly much more that goes into the scouting process than just watching the on-ice actions. As S10 adamantly stated:

> You really need to obtain a complete picture, or the most complete picture that you possibly can because, I think it's critically important. For any young scout that's coming into our world and they come to a hockey rink and then they say, 'Oh look at that guy, he just scored a hat trick and he's really good as a player,' but then you say to him, 'Well I don't know, there's a lot more to what we do than just coming out and watching a game on the ice. That's a starting point for sure, but if you wanna be effective in our world, you have to be like almost a life scout as opposed to a hockey scout.'

These continuous investigative efforts are designed to provide each club with the information they require to make a proper evaluation of a prospect's intangibles.

The research results revealed two distinct types of intangibles that scouts look for in a prospect. The first, enhancing intangibles, focuses on a player's compete level, character, leadership, ability to put the team first, and a passion for the game. Conversely, diminishing intangibles often raised red flags that created questions about a player lacking any of the enhancing intangibles, displaying poor body language or selfish behaviour, and undesirable behaviours from a prospect's parents. The importance of intangible characteristics came to the fore during WHL draft preparations when teams considered the playing ability of a draft prospect in conjunction with the enhancing and diminishing intangibles that had been identified throughout the evaluation process. In many instances, intangible characteristics became a factor within the context of the current organizational culture and existing social dynamics of the teams that individual scouts in the research represented. In addition to having the necessary playing ability, scouts also noted that teams wanted to draft players who were well-rounded citizens and would best represent the team, or brand, in a positive fashion.

At times, a lack of enhancing intangibles or the presence of certain diminishing intangibles seemed to play a larger role or have a stronger negative impact, which often outweighed the physical, technical, and tactical abilities of a draft prospect. The result of a skilled player that consistently exhibited questionable intangibles could lead to the prospect being assigned a lower rank, or outright removal from a team's respective draft list. Several scouts also felt that the most elite players according to their physical, technical, and tactical abilities at that specific age were normally selected in the earliest stages of the draft (i.e., in the first two rounds). After these early rounds were over and the supposed top players were selected, an organization then relied more on intangibles, or the "best person" for the organization, when deciding upon players with comparable talent or skill. The consideration given to intangible player characteristics plays a relevant role in the talent identification process that major junior hockey teams use to determine the draft status of available prospects each year. Overall, the research results regarding diminishing intangibles support the findings of previous academic research that have shown how evaluators make selection or deselection decisions about players making or not making teams. It also coincides with previous research that has shown that evaluators tasked with making team personnel decisions often rely on more than just the physical, technical, and tactical abilities of players when attempting to predict how impactful athletes might be at the next level of competition (Holt & Dunn, 2004; Kavekar & Ford, 2010; Neely et al., 2016; Solomon, 2008).

Notably, an actual operational definition of "intangibles" does not exist within any academic literature, but perhaps this could be a future evolution of TiD research as it relates to intangibles. This is important to make clear as the U of A research that preceded this book was not an attempt to operationally define sport intangibles. Instead, as the title of the research indicates, the study was an exploration into the intangibles that junior hockey scouts consider when evaluating draft-eligible prospects. That said, the majority of enhancing intangible player characteristics, including compete, character, leadership/team player, and passion, that were cited by junior hockey scouts in our study had also been cited in previous research. While the results were not an exact match, the enhancing intangibles uncovered by junior hockey scouts revealed a high degree of overlap with the three previous studies. Referring to the study of NCAA Division 1 softball coaches, Kavekar and Ford (2010) cited being a team player, possessing a strong work ethic, character, hustle, drive, and determination as "intangible characteristics [that] describe a top recruit" (p. 3). Australian youth soccer coaches and club technical directors who participated in a study by Larkin and O'Connor (2017) cited positive attitude (e.g., how players handle disappointment), being competitive (e.g., desire, hunger, and being strong-willed), and character (e.g., disciplined, hard-working, and winning the right way), as important player attributes that were sought in their top prospects. Similarly, in a study of 18 NCAA Division 1, head coaches from various intercollegiate sport programs Solomon and Rhea (2008) cited:

- work ethic, including competitiveness;
- team qualities, including leadership and team chemistry; and
- character, including integrity, trust, and respect.

Again, these were among the "more difficult to 'see' personality factors" (p. 263) that coaches considered when assessing their recruits. Clearly, there are threads of similarities between these studies that seem to indicate certain attributes are consistently part of the evaluation process when making decisions about players to recruit or select. Interestingly, the attributes of character and compete (i.e., consistent work ethic) are found within all three studies, either labelled as personality factors, desirable characteristics, or intangibles. Is it really that simple if you have the playing ability and talent—work hard, be a good person, and you are destined to become a professional athlete? Probably not, but as a parent myself, those seem like great attributes for my daughter to strive and work toward in her own endeavours. Regarding coaches' and evaluators' decisions, it seems plausible that intangibles provide information that they use to predict how much further a player is willing and capable of progressing in their respective sports. If physical, technical, and tactical skills provide a portrait of the current playing capabilities of an athlete, then it appears intangibles are used as an indicator to determine the future ceiling or limits of a player's true potential. In other words, enhancing intangibles could be used as a predictive guide into that player's future potential, and diminishing intangibles might be used as a guide into a prospect's future limitations or downfall.

Given the similarities to previous research, one could argue that enhancing intangible subthemes (i.e., compete, character, leadership/team player, and passion) have been previously identified as positive indicators of future success. However, it is important to note that the labels assigned by evaluators and researchers to capture intangible player characteristics can often mean different things to different people. For example, S7 specifically noted, "Character means different things to different people or different scouts." To junior hockey scouts, character was clearly considered to be an important enhancing intangible, given that 14 of the 16 participants specifically cited this attribute. More specifically, character reflected attributes that were based upon different social, psychological, emotional, behavioural, and moral characteristics that primarily described "the person beyond the hockey player." In contrast, in the research by Larkin and O'Connor (2017), character was defined as representing a player who was "disciplined; [a] hard worker; [and who] wants to win in the right way." In yet another definition, Solomon and Rhea (2008) described character as a prospect that exemplified the five attributes of integrity, courage, trust, honesty, and respect. These five attributes seem to be closely aligned with the positive youth development model whereby character is an outcome and benefit of youth participation in sport (Lerner et al., 2011). Despite a lack of consistency regarding a clear definition of character, the collective commentary from junior hockey scouts taking part in our research describes different overt player behaviours that scouts associate with "good" character in minor hockey players. In simpler terms, the outline of character in this case suggests that a prospect is not "just a hockey player," but a person that has more to contribute to the organization than what gets accomplished on the ice. Still, the inconsistency of terminology and labelling does present problems for theorists, researchers, and practitioners who might be interested in identifying desirable intangible characteristics of potential recruits or drafts.

Quickly for academic readers—from a theoretical perspective, having several definitions can cause measurement problems when researchers use the same label when referencing different constructs/characteristics, or vice versa (Marsh, 1994). This makes it difficult, if not impossible, to successfully advance the systematic study of any psychological construct or phenomenon—in this case, intangible player characteristics—if different researchers use the same label or terminology to describe different ideas. These pitfalls become deeper when researchers try to develop any kind of self or observer report instrument to measure a construct without a proper definition. In simpler terms, if the research community wants to effectively implement and measure intangibles (e.g., in the particular case of character) in the TiD field, then a more standard or operational definition will greatly assist the creation of tools to assess the construct of character.

From an applied perspective, having a clear definition of intangibles, or providing one, is critical for effective use within the field of talent identification. For example, if members of a scouting staff have been directed by their general manager or director of scouting to find players with "good character," but are presented with no clear understanding of what that means, then there is likely to be confusion between the judgements of scouts and the GM about the character of a player. This lack of clarity could have a harmful effect upon the success of talent identification and draft processes within an organization, but also could lead to the scouting staff choosing players that do not fit with the desired culture or team dynamic that is sought by an organization. Going back to the comments provided by our CE in Chapter 9, the scouting staff has a big influence over which players are selected, but after draft day their interactions with any draft selection is limited. If character is misinterpreted or improperly factored into a draft selection by the scouting staff and the person behind the player turns out to be rotten, then the rest of the staff (i.e., executive staff, coaches, development personnel, administrative staff) are stuck with the dud! The value of having a consistent and clear "mission" regarding personnel selection has been recognized within some of the largest modern-day organizations. Take Google for example, a highly successful and globally recognizable technology company. As noted by Lazlo Block, Google's senior vice president of people operations, the corporate culture has been built around people who are passionate, adaptable, and those who crave knowledge (Hammel & Kleiner, 2015). Block's strategy for organizational success begins with hiring the right people. "Before you start recruiting, decide what attributes you want and define as a group what great looks like" (Feloni, 2015). Define what looks great—I really like that at as a starting point. If researchers and practitioners (e.g., scouts, evaluators in the field) want to better understand intangible player characteristics in sport, then it might make sense to develop clear operational definitions or construct labels that have the same meaning and reflect the same characteristics to all people across studies/contexts. This would be an exciting project, but I will leave that up to folks far smarter than me to make the attempt—this book and research will hopefully get the ball rolling a little faster. At the very minimum, I would recommend sporting organizations to clearly articulate and regularly review the important intangibles they seek in a prospect according to their cultural norms, values, standards, etc.

Given that the current study was conducted in a team sport setting, it does not seem surprising that the junior hockey scouts identified leadership and being a team player as desirable intangible characteristics that enhance the draft status of players. Players displaying leadership qualities were generally described by scouts as those who were adjudged to be mature role models both on and off the ice, as well as individuals that demonstrate the ability to positively influence their teammates. It is plausible that the scouts may be referring to players who have comparatively high levels of emotional intelligence within their peer group. Prior research suggests that players that have comparatively high levels of emotional intelligence within their peer group can make better leaders at the next level (Salovey & Mayer, 1990). As previously noted, young players at the bantam (U15) age will likely be all over the proverbial map in terms of emotional maturity levels. However, the one skill that can be consistently reinforced, especially from home, is to put the team's needs ahead of their own—the younger this starts, the better. It stands to reason that top-end players participating in team sports that consistently put the team's needs ahead of their own become natural leaders, and only become more valuable as they mature—even if they are not necessarily the best players at the next level of competition. Prior research has shown that a team-first attitude, or being a good team player, has been identified as a specific player attribute that coaches in British soccer academies felt was required to reach the professional level of the sport (Mills et al., 2012), and has also been associated with superior performance in NFL players (Whiting & Maynes, 2016). Research at the highest levels of international team sport supports this view—successful and resilient teams are made up of players who are willing to do nearly anything for their team, regardless of the personal cost, if the action is believed to help the team achieve its goals (Morgan, Fletcher, & Sarkar, 2015). Team-first behaviours, leadership qualities, and emotional maturity have been identified in previous studies examining desirable intangible player characteristics that are sought by coaches when evaluating and selecting players for their teams (Kavekar & Ford, 2017; Solomon, 2008; Solomon & Rhea, 2008). The supporting evidence in favour of players who put the team first is substantial. Junior hockey scouts in our U of A study underlined prior evidence by placing a premium on players that put the needs of the team ahead of their own and do whatever is needed to win, clearly stated by S4: "A guy that'll do anything to win, like doesn't matter what it is, they'll do it to win."

Having genuine passion, enthusiasm, and love for the game of hockey was the final intangible characteristic junior hockey scouts frequently cited as an important attribute that enhanced the draft status of eligible prospects. While it is an intangible that can be difficult to measure precisely, passion has been proven to be an invaluable characteristic for athletes to prevail over setbacks that they will inevitably face. A love of the game has been identified as an important intangible athlete characteristic that is valued by coaches and selectors in various sport settings (Holt & Dunn, 2004; Larkin & O'Connor, 2017; Solomon, 2008; Solomon & Rhea, 2008). One scout in our study suggested that he felt passion was essential for players to succeed at the next level of competition, because the demands of the sport (e.g., time, effort, travel, training, social expectations, physical toll, speed of the game, etc.) only increase as an individual advances to the next level of competition (i.e., the WHL). These increasing demands at higher levels of any competitive sport can create heightened levels of stress that can lead to elevated instances of burnout and emotional exhaustion for some athletes (Cresswell & Eklund, 2006).

Often, passion is related to the true motivation and driving factor of why an athlete continues to play the game. Previous research with young swimmers (Raedeke, 1997) showed that athletes who swam for internally driven attraction-related reasons (e.g., enjoyment and love of their sport) tended to have lower burnout scores than athletes who competed for more extrinsically imposed reasons (e.g., to avoid a loss of identity or "the jacket"). Thus, passion or love of the game can provide an athlete with the motivation and internal drive that provides the necessary energy—whether it be physical, psychological, or emotional—for continuous "engagement in highly demanding activities" (Vallerand et al., 2008) and to remain committed (Holt & Dunn, 2004) with a high work ethic (Solomon & Rhea, 2008) in the pursuit of athletic excellence. The most precise way to measure passion and intrinsic motivation would be the use of self-report measures which are frequently referred to in sport psychology literature (Saw, Main, Robertson, & Gastin, 2017; Verner-Filion, Vallerand, Amiot, & Mocanu, 2017). However, from the U of A interviews, it appeared that many scouts believed they could identify a player's passion and love of the game based upon the perception of a player's overt behaviours on or off the ice, as well as from information gathered through the investigative efforts (e.g., interviews with players, parents, coaches, trainers and/or questionnaire responses). To examine the accuracy of a group of scout's subjective assessment of player passion would make for interesting future research, but it seems reasonable to think that a scout's tacit knowledge (i.e., knowledge gathered through years of scouting experience) combined with observation/investigative information could provide some level of accuracy in measuring passion.

After years of scouting young players, I feel that the passion of a prospect can be seen after multiple viewings, and the information collected off the ice normally solidifies whether those observations are accurate or just a good acting job.

Diminishing Intangibles Review

A unique aspect of the junior hockey research was the emergence of themes that reflected diminishing intangibles (i.e., characteristics or attributes that could diminish the draft status of an eligible player). Academically speaking, the discovery of these negative intangibles deviates from previous research that has examined intangible characteristics of players who are being considered for selection to play at the next level (e.g., Kavekar & Ford, 2010; Larkin & O'Connor, 2017; Solomon, 2008; Solomon & Rhea, 2008). This finding represents an important contribution to the research community, as well as the common perception of intangibles. In both instances, intangibles are normally referred to in a positive light. Within the popular media, the term "intangible" often infers good qualities about athletes, and that having intangibles should be revered. By asking scouts to identify characteristics that could make them hesitant about drafting players that exhibit intangibles provided viable and ample information. Any prior research only offered answers that followed questions which solely focused upon the identification of intangible characteristics that enhance a player's draft status or overall evaluation. For example, no participants mentioned anything about parental behaviours when asked to discuss intangible characteristics that would help a player's evaluation, but 11 of the 16 participants specifically mentioned poor parent behaviour as something that would hurt the draft status of a player.

This reverse line of questioning regarding intangibles proved fruitful, as it proves to young athletes that scouts, coaches, and other evaluators are indeed noticing these negative behaviours, attributes, or characteristics. In fact, for many scouts and their respective organizations, the identification of certain diminishing intangibles, often referred to as "red flags," commonly outweighed the presence of enhancing intangibles resulting in a net negative evaluation of a prospect. Thus, diminishing intangibles do not simply represent the absence of enhancing intangibles (i.e., a lack of passion, character, compete, or a lack of leadership and not being a team player), but also appear to contribute in their own unique and meaningful way to the overall evaluation process. Given the prominent role diminishing intangibles appear to play in the evaluation of draft prospects, future research should explore both enhancing intangibles and diminishing intangibles that can influence decision-making criteria that coaches, scouts, and evaluators consider when selecting or not selecting athletes at various levels of competition. Further, if diminishing intangibles can have a large impact on a player's future, this also presents a valuable learning opportunity for coaches, parents, and young athletes. The recommended age would depend on the sport and corresponding talent identification efforts, but in my estimation a good age range might be close to the end of the FUNdamentals stage before an athlete enters the Learn to Train stage, based on most Long-term Athlete Development models. In other words, children aged 8–10 could benefit from learning more about the importance of both enhancing and diminishing intangibles.

Within the diminishing intangibles theme were four sub-themes labelled lack of enhancers, poor body language, selfish behaviour, and poor parental behaviour. All 16 scouts noted that a player having a large deficiency in a specific enhancing intangible (i.e., compete, character, leadership/team player, or passion) would diminish a player's draft status. This intangible strongly reinforces the importance of enhancing intangibles during the evaluation process. A large absence of a specific enhancing intangible clearly raised concerns for scouts regarding the ability of a player to fulfill the needs of their organization as much as the presence of specific diminishing intangibles, such as poor body language, selfish behaviour, or poor parental behaviour.

Poor body language was cited by 14 scouts as a diminishing intangible. Over the last several decades, applied sport psychologists have recognized the importance of teaching athletes to be aware of their body language and how body language can convey wanted or unwanted information to teammates, opponents, and/or coaches (Halliwell, 1989). After recording observations of body language, researchers noted how these messages could provide insight into the "self-confidence, motivation, and emotional stability" (Taylor, 1995, p. 343) of an athlete. Another study with competitive female curling athletes ages 23–58 identified the ability to control one's overt body language, especially when players were angry, as a critical aspect of emotional self-control that was necessary to prevent the non-verbal communication of unwanted or destructive messages to teammates (Tamminen & Crocker, 2013). Similarly, instances of poor body language by players (e.g., banging a stick, excessive swearing, ignoring in-game meetings/instruction, anger toward own teammates/coaches) following situations of personal or team adversity was viewed by scouts as a response that might indicate a larger issue surrounding a lack of emotional maturity or emotional intelligence. Repeated displays of these antics were considered poor body language and could potentially result in a prospect being labelled with a red flag on a scouting staff's respective draft list. The evidence presented herein should provide enough support the notion that young hockey players might benefit from educational sport psychology programs that teach them:

- the importance of consciously controlling their body language before, during, and after competition; and
- how such control might ultimately influence their own performance (Halliwell, 1989), the performance of their teammates (Tamminen & Crocker, 2013), as well as the impressions they leave with coaches (Larkin & O'Connor, 2017) and scouts who play a role in determining whether or not the athlete is selected to compete at higher levels of competition.

Selfish behaviour, the antithesis of being a team player, was specifically mentioned by 11 scouts during the interview stage, and was a detriment to a prospect's draft status. Labelling a lack of enhancers (specifically in this case, a lack of team play) and selfishness as separate diminishing intangibles might seem unnecessary, but it seemed too prevalent a theme to ignore—that, and overt acts of selfish behaviour were met with disdain and disgust by several scouts. For example, one context-specific attribute that reflected selfish behaviour was termed "chiseling." Chiseling happens when a player tries to rack up more points and recognition by passing along their own number to referees following an offensive play in which the player did not actually contribute to the play, and hence did not even deserve the point (i.e., goal or assist). Chiseling is often very easy for scouts to see, and there is no better—or worse—way that a player could exemplify behaviours that are the exact opposite of being a team player. That said, in no instances did scouts indicate that chiseling had any immediate negative impact upon the team during competition. Instead, chiseling was viewed as a character flaw that gave scouts the impression that the player lacked integrity or honesty, and might therefore lose the trust of teammates. If selfish actions are easily noticed by outside observers, then I can almost guarantee that teammates not only clearly see through that behaviour, they also likely despise it. Once teammates start to question whether a player will do the right thing or help the team in the future, trust is very hard to retain (Solomon & Rhea, 2008). Thus, chiseling, or any other type of behaviour that is deemed to be selfish, can "damage a player's value in the eyes of peers, fans … coaches [and scouts]" (Uhlmann & Barnes, 2014, p. 4), and has the potential to undermine the level of trust between players that is necessary for effective team performance (Martin, Wilson, Evans, & Spink, 2015). Again, this creates another excellent opportunity to educate young hockey players and/or their parents about the pitfalls of selfish behaviour. By simply informing young players that although they might think they are helping their status by accumulating more offensive points, such actions could develop into bad habits that might undermine their progress down the road. Again, my own opinion is that this selfish obsession with points has become a sickness in the game of hockey, and it seems like this behaviour starts to creep into players' psyche at an early age. While creating offence is the name of the game in sports, individual players should not prioritize their own production over the team's efforts, because it can often become an unwanted distraction. Selfishness can often breed more selfish behaviour and can result in a team becoming just a group of individuals without any collaborative purpose.

The final diminishing intangible is a well-documented and publicized phenomena of youth sport—poor parental behaviour. Eleven of 16 scouts commented upon parental behaviour that could diminish the draft status of a player. The role of parental behaviour in youth sport has generated a considerable amount of research within sport psychology literature (e.g., Holt & Knight, 2014; Jeffery-Tosoni, Fraser-Thomas & Baker, 2014; Knight, Berrow, & Harwood, 2017; Knight, Neely & Holt, 2011) as poor parental behaviour during competitions (e.g., criticizing or yelling at officials, verbal or physical altercations with opposing parents) has been identified as a source of unwanted stress on many different levels, but especially for young athletes (Elliott & Drummond, 2017; Jeffery-Tosoni et al., 2014). Coaches have also discussed the damaging influence that parental behaviour can have on the athletic development of young athletes. Several research examples of parental behaviour that have been recognized as disruptive or destructive include parents that direct anger/complaints towards coaches, conditional emotional support of the athlete based on parental expectations, and the dreaded "parent coach" instruction, which normally contradicts the real coach's instruction (Bean, Jeffery-Tosoni, Fraser-Thomas, & Baker, 2016; Elliott & Drummond, 2017; Ross, Mallett, & Parkes, 2015). Other examples cited in academic studies, or by the media, have exposed parents verbally abusing officials, opposing players, and parents of opposing teams (Jeffery-Tosoni et al., 2014). Despite the abundance of literature highlighting problems in Canadian youth hockey surrounding the actions of parents, our junior hockey study is the first to provide direct evidence from scouts that many of these unruly parental behaviours could negatively impact the evaluation of a young hockey player wanting to be selected to compete at a higher level of competition. Further, the veracity in which some scouts made claims was noteworthy—several were adamant that they simply would not consider drafting a player whose parents acted in unruly ways, regardless of how athletically talented the player might be. This might open yet another opportunity to develop, implement, and assess parental education programs in youth hockey, and in organized youth sport more generally (Bean et al., 2016; Dorsch, King, Dunn, Osai, & Tulane, 2017). Programs might outline the negative impact certain parental behaviours can have on their children's' future playing opportunities, as well as providing illustrations of exemplary parents in sport (Pynn, S., Dunn, J. G. H., & Holt, N. L, 2019).

From my own perspective, it seems as though parents of young athletes often get inundated with information and examples of terrible parenting. An alternative approach might be a combined effort in providing information on how a parent can destroy the image of their own child, but also providing examples of what great parenting looks like. This could prove to be especially effective if parents of young athletes are offered examples from the parents of current and recognizable professional players—kind of like providing a role model for parents.

It should be evident that enhancing and diminishing intangibles play a role in helping scouting staffs generate the final draft list for each player the organization has been considering throughout the process. A number of scouts indicated that diminishing intangibles were particularly important when ranking top-end prospects (i.e., highly skilled, talented players) if a player had continually exhibited or been proven to possess specific attribute(s) that led to a staff assigning the prospect with red flags. Prospects labelled with red flags would often create concern amongst staff members about the potential negative impact a prospect could have on the team or organization in the future. Several scouts also noted the important role that intangibles played in the middle to later rounds of the draft when most of the physically talented players, at the U15 age, had likely already been selected. At these later stages of the draft, scouts indicated that most of the undrafted players were quite similar in terms of their physical and playing capabilities, which meant the intangible characteristics played a more prominent role in determining which players would be drafted by their respective organization. A similar approach was also used by head coaches of provincial-select youth sport teams when deciding whether to select or deselect the so-called "fringe players" in their squads (Neely et al., 2016). The existence of enhancing or diminishing intangibles seemed to play a crucial role within talent identification and scouting when tie-breaking decisions were required to choose between players who possessed similar playing abilities.

Chapter 11
FAQ: Routes

AS A JUNIOR HOCKEY SCOUT AND MENTAL PERFORMANCE CON-
sultant, I receive many different inquiries by parents and prospects
alike. Earlier I mentioned that one of the most frequently asked questions
by young players is: How do I get noticed? Of course, my answer is always:
Win. Less talented players that do whatever is necessary or asked of them
to help his/her team win will always earn the respect of evaluators and get
"second, third looks" as a result. Further, if a less talented player consistently
contributes to the success of a championship team then that prospect will
likely get plenty of opportunities to play at higher levels of competition. In
fact, this winning concept resonates with the entire message of this book—a
less talented player that competes, has a passion for winning, is a great teammate and person will succeed in sport and in life. Of course, this message
is equally important to highly talented players—think Kobe and his 13th
player mindset at Lower Merion High School.

All that said, there are two specific parent questions that I am most
frequently asked to provide my answers or perspective on, and this short
chapter will provide insight on those queries. As such, the answers will be
written more like an experiential opinion piece more than a factually driven
research response. Another caveat is that these questions and answers, especially the first one, will be most relevant for hockey prospects located in
Western Canada.

Question #1: *What is the best route for my draft-eligible (i.e., WHL age)
son? In other words, should he continue playing within the local minor hockey
system, or attend an academy to play in the Canadian Sport School Hockey
League (CSSHL)?*

Any decision in life will have pros and cons attached to the final choice,
but once a decision is made, the goal is to make the best of any situation.
In other words, whatever route you as a family decide upon will have some

good times, but will also likely run into some adversity along the way. In my opinion, that is one of our main responsibilities as a parent—to help our children deal with and overcome adversity—not to point fingers and blame shortcomings on teammates, or the coaching staff, or the league if things do not go our way. **Instead, we do what we can to make the best of a situation no matter what we encounter.** Philosophers might argue that this "truth in suffering" is a basic tenet of the human condition, and it is where we as humans grow the most, by learning from and overcoming failure.

Realistically, the first question a family should ask themselves is: Can we *truly* afford an academy? Not: Can we cut some costs out of the budget, or save up over the summer, or mortgage the family home so that we can afford the academy? Can we comfortably afford this option? If the answer is yes, no problem; awesome. The academy system is a great development system. However, if a family decides to send their son or daughter to an academy, but have mortgaged their future to do it, that is where things can go horribly wrong. Again, any young player is going to have good and bad stretches during a season at any level, so how mom or dad reacts when a young athlete underperforms has short- and long-term ramifications. If the parent's response is to put more pressure on the child to perform, then that can become a recipe for disaster. In the short-term, that kind of pressure can lead to even steeper performance declines and can also drive a young athlete out of the sport. Over the long term, the resulting resentment, from both sides, can create a toxic child/parent relationship. At the end of the day, if your family can comfortably afford the CSSHL/academy league, then it is a great place to develop young hockey players. Over the last decade (since 2010 or so), the CSSHL has become the premiere league for U15 age players and each year they produce not only the most talent, but also some of the top talent available in the WHL draft. Please note, that does not mean *all* of the top talent.

There are many reasons why the academy level is attractive for parents and young players alike. In my opinion, there are three primary factors that contribute to the overall success of the academy model:

1. The training, instruction, and coaching players receive.
2. The day-to-day, game-to-game competition.
3. The preparation.

The biggest differentiator of the academy model is the off-ice/on-ice training instruction the players receive. Again, this is only my opinion, but the main reason that academy players receive better or more detailed instruction is because coaches or trainers are being paid a full-time salary! In comparison, most minor hockey coaches might get a small stipend throughout the season, and any amount they do receive usually pales in comparison to the effort that they put forth. That alone is a huge factor in the attraction and retention of top coaches, trainers, and ancillary staff available. Are there exceptions to this generality? Of course. Some minor hockey teams have fantastic coaches that give away their time, dedication, and effort because they love the game, just like there are a few academy coaches that might not be worth the cheque they receive every two weeks. Generally, if you are a good coach and someone is willing to pay you for your time, expertise, and effort, then it may be tempting to get paid accordingly. Conversely, a quality minor hockey coach who is being paid in rubles may just say "no thanks" to the continuous demands and entitlement that are an accepted part of today's game. When, and likely not if, that minor hockey coach calls it quits, are they being replaced by less capable staff? In the big picture, academy players get superior coaching based on compensation alone.

As the CSSHL has become a desired destination for players and families, it subsequently attracts the most depth in terms of talent. For example, a handful of the best academy teams each season may have both goalies, the entire defence corps, and 8 of 12 forwards be drafted. This might be the biggest contrast between the two avenues: most academy teams have a greater concentration of talent compared to minor hockey teams where only two to three players from a team may get drafted. Is that talent necessarily better? For me, the talent is always close in terms of the top-end eligible players, but the academies just have more prospects per team. This eventually translates into academy players going up against the best competition, not only in games, but also in day-to-day practice sessions as well. At such a crucial developmental age, players that compete against the best players in their peer group on a consistent basis will normally improve at a faster rate.

This increased competitive factor at the academy level also seems to prepare young players for the consistency they will require to compete at the next level of play. The quality of instruction along with consistent high calibre competition also prepares athletes for what they can expect in terms of regimented schedules and demands at the next level of play. In some cases, academy players leave home for the first time to play in a larger centre, so they are inherently more prepared to move away, depending on which junior franchise drafts them. Is this always the best scenario? Not by a long shot. In fact, some young players that experience a highly regimented schedule at a young age are susceptible to burnout later in their junior career. Another consideration is that academy players might be as polished as they will ever get coming out of that league, and their individual improvement rate slows down, whereas minor hockey players might pass them by when they are required to do more of what will make them successful.

In the end, there is no right or wrong answer to the question. Make a sound, solid decision that is in the best interest of the player and the family, then make the best of the situation. The draft year is built up as a be-all and end-all season, but believe me, it is not. In fact, whether a player is a first rounder, 10th rounder, or not drafted really does not matter once the next season starts. The fact is, every player will still need to put in a tremendous amount of work to continue getting better each day. For every Rick Rypien, there are plenty of examples where first-round picks could not handle the spotlight or do not put in the required effort because they are already "the man," and they slowly fade out of the game. The player and the family that have a long-term, more reasonable perspective and focus are those that concentrate on what they can control: competing each day, being a good teammate, loving what they do, and being a good person. The rest, whatever that might entail within hockey, sport, or life, usually takes care of itself.

Question #2: *What is the best route for my son: major junior (e.g., WHL, OHL, QMJHL) or junior A/NCAA?*

The divisive landscape between major junior and junior A/NCAA hockey is one of the more hotly contested debates within amateur hockey in North American. Obviously, my natural bias is toward the WHL, but I would also like to think of myself as a scholar that can objectively comment on the debate. The fact is, both avenues provide a great setting for the overall development of a young player, and each route will suit some players better than others. That said, the competition for the game's brightest talent has never been fiercer, and like the minor hockey vs. academy debate, whichever route a family chooses will unquestionably come with some peaks and valleys accordingly.

The contentiousness of this debate is exasperated by the restrictive NCAA regulations regarding how that athletic body recognizes the three leagues (WHL, OHL, QMJHL) that make up the CHL. Below you can see a brief WHL interpretation of the NCAA rules under the FAQ section of the WHL's prospect page:

There are three ways NCAA eligibility can be affected when it comes to the WHL. According to NCAA rules, they are as follows:

1. *A player signs a WHL Standard Player Agreement.*

2. *A player participates in a WHL pre-season, regular season, or playoff game.*

3. *A player remains in a WHL training camp for more than 48 hours at the club's expense. Please note that if a player's family pays for any costs after the 48-hour period, a player can remain in a WHL camp for as long as they want.*

Players can still attend WHL training camps, talk with WHL general managers, coaches, and scouts, and visit WHL club facilities without having any impact on their NCAA eligibility.

This is not to point the proverbial finger at the NCAA; it just is what is and has been for a long time. The fact is, if a young player wants to keep his NCAA eligibility, then he cannot take part in any kind of WHL, OHL, or QMJHL game—not even an exhibition game. These regulations play a factor in each WHL training camp when both the prospect, his parents, and the team in question will reach a critical juncture where all parties want to see how a player fits in at the WHL level of play. The best way to judge the readiness of a prospect is during the pre-season (i.e., exhibition games) when rosters consist of a balanced mix between rookies and veterans on each side. However, as per the NCAA rules, participation in any pre-season game cancels a player's college eligibility. This forces the prospect and his family into making an ultimate decision about the player's future at the age of 16 or

17, or younger—something that many folks struggle with and hence it being a frequently asked question.

As a household rule, when I was learning how to make these kinds of decisions as a young man, my parents would always encourage me to write out a pros/cons list. There are several pros/cons that athletes and families must first be aware of before they can make the right choice for them. What might be considered an advantage for one athlete and family might be perceived as a constraint for another. That said, it would be irrational and irresponsible for me to attempt a pros/cons list for each potential route, because many of the considerations will depend on the perception of the athlete and his family. Instead, I will provide a list of considerations so that families can create their own pros/cons list, as well as a few corresponding questions to ask scouts, recruiters, and executives along the way:

- **Scholarship status.** Both avenues offer excellent scholarship packages, but is the scholarship money guaranteed? Are there conditions or time constraints attached with scholarship money? Is a full scholarship guaranteed or is it re-evaluated on a year-by-year basis?
- **Length of season/schedule.** Is a shorter or longer schedule best for your son? Junior players are exposed to a longer, more pro-like schedule, while the NCAA season is shorter and more compact. Some individuals might consider the longer season better, while others might say a shorter schedule keeps players fresh (e.g., fewer injuries, more energy, more time to train, etc.).
- **Course load.** Is my son able to handle a full engineering or pre-medical load while playing at this level? Players that have completed high school are eligible to take university courses in both scenarios.
- **Situational or staff changes.** As noted, hockey staffs have a higher turnover rate, so what happens if a new coach or manager enters the program after we have already committed to the organization? Can I move schools or be traded if this new situation does not work out?
- **NHL signing rights.** What happens if my son is drafted by an NHL team? Are there any time constraints that may be an advantage or disadvantage for him signing a contract? (Not all players drafted by an NHL team will ever sign a professional contract.)

- **Competition (while at the junior level).** What is the level of competition while he is playing at the junior level? Is he going to be playing against the best players in that geographic region?
- **Development.** What is best for my son: to play against the best competition as soon as possible or gradually allow him to develop over a longer trajectory (i.e., is your son ready physically and developed as such, or could he be a late bloomer)?
- **Eligibility.** This has been covered earlier, but there are other small nuances that players bound for the NCAA should also know in terms of expenses: what they can or cannot accept, etc. Conversely, does an NCAA player lose his major junior eligibility at any point?
- **Organization/culture.** From the contents of this book, I could not leave this part out of the equation! What kind of impression do you have about the organization/institution? Are you comfortable and do you trust the people and members that make up the organization? What kind of history does the club have in terms of winning championships? Does the institution have a track record of producing NHL talent?

Obviously, there are many considerations for a young man to ponder before making this tough decision, but it also prepares that young athlete to think critically about his future. It also teaches a young man to live with the ultimate decision and can help them realize that no decision we ever make in life will be perfect. There are going to be strikes and gutters every which way we go, but our pursuit should always be to make the best of any situation. At the end of the day, both routes have produced many top-end professional players, and provide excellent educational benefits along the way. However, it is up to each family to decide what is best for them, and I hope the above considerations can offer some assistance during the deliberation process.

Chapter 12
Final Thoughts

A PPROPRIATE RESEARCH METHODS WERE USED TO GENERATE the contents of this book, but there are several factors readers should consider regarding the results. As previously stated, the goal of this book was to provide information that could potentially assist researchers, as well as scouts, parents, and athletes involved in youth sport. More specifically, the results provide valuable information that expand upon the current knowledge of the what, why, and how questions regarding intangible characteristics used to evaluate youth athletes and specifically junior hockey prospects. However, before the results of the research can be appropriately or correctly applied in other sport domains, the following key limitations must be considered:

- the degree to which the results can be applied to non-contact sports;
- practical application differences between individual vs. team sports;
- how results might vary based on gender of player and/or evaluator; and
- the overall accuracy of participating scout evaluations.

Whether the results from our U of A research with junior hockey scouts can be applied beyond the specific context of elite level male youth hockey in Canada is unknown. Despite the reduction in physicality over the past several decades, hockey is still considered a high-contact team sport, therefore the degree to which information could be applied to non-contact team sports also remains undetermined. These same questions can be applied to how useful information regarding intangible characteristics might be for athletes that excel within individual sport versus team sport. From a sport psychology perspective, there are valuable, practical lessons that can be applied from team to individual sport, and vice versa, but there are also obvious differences between the two types of activities. Similarly, all participants within the research (i.e., scouts) were male, and the athletes they were evaluating were male, making it entirely possible that different intangible characteristics may have been generated if the study had been conducted with female evaluators who assessed female athletes. Sport research has long recognized the difference between male and female athlete preferences toward the leadership behaviours of coaches (Chelladurai, & Saleh, 1978), and differences between preferences for certain types of leadership behaviours between male and female athletes based upon the gender of their coaches (Reimer & Toon, 2001). It therefore seems quite possible that male and female evaluators/scouts/coaches/selectors in sport may perceive leadership characteristics differently, and look for different leadership intangibles when evaluating potential recruits. Additionally, organizational psychology literature underscores the existence of gender differences in the way male and female interviewers assess candidates during job interviews (Chapman & Rowe, 2001). Considering this evidence, it would seem sensible to account for the gender of both the evaluator and the athlete when examining intangible player characteristics in the talent identification process. Another note regarding the participants is the fact that no attempt was made to properly assess, or gauge, the degree to which scouts had made correct historical decisions about players they had identified as suitable draft picks for their respective organizations. In other words, it cannot be inferred that the junior hockey scouts participating in the U of A research were correct in their evaluations, or even which intangible player characteristics truly contributed to the long-term success of draft picks and their teams. Frankly, the same could be said about my own opinions, ideas, or contributions to the evaluation of enhancing and diminishing intangibles. However, it seems unlikely that WHL teams would continue to employ scouts, all of whom had more than five years of WHL experience—and collectively had amassed 265 years of total junior hockey scouting experience—if they did not believe that their ongoing recommendations regarding draft prospects were not contributing to the success of their respective organizations. Further, having had the opportunity to interview 16 highly experienced junior hockey scouts, and using standardized interview guidelines, was a huge bonus for the research team. Not to mention, the application of sound research methods to gather and analyze the information to generate the results suggests a degree of reliability within the data. Like most qualitative research efforts, the only way to genuinely verify these results would likely require the use of longitudinal research. A study of this magnitude would need to systematically document and evaluate draft picks based on their intangible characteristics as judged by a scout, or group of scouts, prior to each successive draft. Researchers would then need to track the progress and performance of players throughout their WHL careers and beyond (e.g., intercollegiate hockey or professional hockey). This could help solidify which of the intangible player characteristics were more, or less, strongly associated with the career development of athletes that compete in sports employing a draft process. Believe me when I say that this would be a fascinating project to be part of, and research that *could* provide breakthrough information for talent identification research in sport. The key word in that sentence is *could*, and certainly not a guarantee. Longitudinal studies have proven to be extremely costly ventures that require major funding to properly execute and complete making this more of a pipe dream than a potential reality. However, if any readers are interested in funding such a project, I would be all ears!

Based on academic research results, this book has established the important role intangible characteristics play in the evaluation process used by junior hockey scouts to assess the draft suitability of minor hockey players in Western Canada. This book outlines an argument in favour of the suggestion that junior hockey scouting staffs consider a wide range of attributes and characteristics during the evaluation process. These attributes, labelled intangibles, have shown that the evaluation of junior hockey prospects extend beyond the performance-based indicators of a player's physical, technical, and tactical abilities. As mentioned by numerous scouts that participated in the research, a high degree of consideration is given to a prospect's character, or the person behind the player. Therefore, it seems reasonable that individuals who play a role in the training and development of young hockey players and athletes (e.g., coaches, parents, support staff, personal trainers, etc.) may want to consider the degree to which their efforts are directed toward teaching youngsters about intangible attributes such as character, leadership, passion, body language, and team-first behaviours. Within the Long-term Player Development Plan for Canadian hockey (Hockey Canada, 2013) there appears to be a predominant focus upon technical, tactical, and physical development of young players. While technical, tactical, and physical skills will always play an essential role in the development of young hockey players, it might be an opportune time to implement additional emphasis upon the aforementioned intangible characteristics that can also enhance the development of young players. If the presence of certain enhancing intangibles (compete, character, teamwork/leadership, passion) or the absence of certain diminishing intangibles (lack of enhancing intangibles, poor body language, selfish behaviour, poor parental behaviour), can help athletes move to the next level of competition, then there may be value in adding this information into the curriculum for the long-term development of young players within the game of hockey.

The intangible player characteristics described in this book generally provide a behavioural reflection of underlying psychological characteristics that are assumed to exist within the players who are being evaluated. It could be argued that many of the psychological characteristics might already be ingrained in athletes by the time they are being scouted for junior, college, or professional levels. However, prior research suggests that the development and implementation of psychological skills (e.g., self-awareness/assessment, goal setting, self-talk, emotional regulation) can help athletes develop or enhance certain psychological characteristics that may be associated with enhancing intangibles (Dohme, Backhouse, Piggott & Morgan, 2017). Logically, the next step in the process is developing a sound approach to effectively deliver the concept of intangibles for young athletes. This could be another avenue for future research, but the creation of any potential curriculum would likely start by addressing two questions regarding intangibles.

The first question is *how?* How can interested parties (e.g., coaches, parents, support staff, personal trainers, etc.) effectively communicate the underlying message from this book in a creative, informative, and effective format? The implementation of age-appropriate psychological skills training during early stages of athletic development is the crossroads where educational programs can help young athletes develop long-term behavioural tendencies that reflect positive psychological characteristics outlined in this book. Meaning, any presentation of information regarding intangibles should ensure the material is suitable and understandable for the intended audience. Personally speaking, my presentation approach is to make the material as interesting and informative as possible by trying to create a unique lens according to the age group. In other words, if my audience is a team of elite U12 hockey players, I might include recognizable figures (e.g., athletes who are globally renown—Usain Bolt, Serena Williams, LeBron James—those that have been on top of the world in their given sport) from different team or individual sports, and then bring the intended message back to hockey. Sport is truly a universal language and every sport offers examples—such as the culture of the All Blacks rugby team, or what it means to unify and then move up a weight division in boxing, or the composure that is required in bull riding—that can provide excellent discussion points about many of the intangibles or implications that arise from within this book. The eventual goal is for the audience to find the information intelligible, but also to engage and capture their collective attention over the appropriate time frame (i.e., anything over 40–45 minutes maximum is probably pushing it for most audiences, no matter the age group). Another rationale for this approach is that I find athletes are inundated and consumed with material or information related to their own sport every day, all day, and year-round. Of course, this is counterintuitive to the intangible of passion, but within hockey it just seems like it is hockey, hockey, and more hockey for these young athletes. In many instances, athletes seem to appreciate learning about relevant information that they can apply to their own sport, but also being exposed to new material that provides a different but useful performance-enhancing perspective. I am belabouring the point, but this is the beauty of sport—no matter what "your" sport is currently, there are always plenty of performance-enhancing material available for young athletes. Further, I think it provides a healthy perspective for players to reflectively view themselves as an athlete instead of identifying as just a hockey player or tennis player or baseball player or boxer, etc. The ability to appreciate the talent and feats that happen across sporting contexts is the origin of an athlete, and one that will be active for life. Just because an athlete may not fulfill their dreams of becoming a professional football/baseball/softball/rugby player does not mean they cannot become an Olympic medallist on the bobsled or on the speed skating track or with the pole vault! One of the most cherished skills I garnished from my graduate studies was this clear ability to watch a sporting event through a completely different lens and be able to apply different concepts to my sport psychology consulting. That said, coaches from an individual sport may be hesitant, or find it meaningless for his or her athlete to learn about the intangibles of being a team player. In response, I might argue that there are always lessons to be learned if you are looking at things through the right lens, and providing a fresh perspective can help an elite individual sport athlete have a breakthrough with a particular mental hurdle they may be encountering. Athletes that participate in elite level individual sports likely know that they require a strong team around them in order for them to fulfill their potential. After all, where would a professional golfer be without their caddy—that is a team, right? Conversely, there are many lessons team sport athletes can learn from individual sport participants. That is the beauty of sport psychology--any type of sport can provide valuable lessons when it is organized and presented in the appropriate manner.

The next strategy for effectively advising young players about long-term benefits of intangibles is by addressing the question of *why?* Historically, young athletes (specifically, hockey players based on my current familiarity and proximity to the sport) were given instructions, and orders were carried out—no questions asked. However, the consensus amongst minor hockey, academy, and junior coaches nowadays is that the current generation of players want to know the *why* behind any actionable instructions provided. *Why* is this drill or activity or information or video clip important for me? In my own opinion, the questioning nature of today's young hockey player is not born out of defiance, but rather curiosity. It is not my place to say whether this is wrong or right, it just is, and personally speaking I would never begrudge a young person for being curious. However, practitioners, coaches, trainers, or managers must accept the reality of that curiosity and adjust communication strategies accordingly. Long gone are the days where young athletes respond to the militaristic and authoritarian coaching styles of the past. If explaining the *why* helps young athletes digest information about intangibles, then we can collectively turn to one of our primary research questions: why are intangibles important to the scouting process? The answer: culture.

As noted, the game of hockey, and likely many other youth sports, has become increasingly driven by the individualistic wants, needs, or desires of players. These individualistic tendencies seem to creep into hockey at a very young age and in many ways shape intangibles that are counterproductive to the long-term development of a player. In other words, individualistic emphasis creates more diminishing intangibles and fewer enhancing intangibles.

In my opinion, one way to reverse this individualistic trend would require a shift toward an emphasis on culture, and relaying that message to young athletes so that they begin to understand what it truly means to be an effective member of a successful team. If hockey and/or sport organizations are genuinely interested in assisting players develop the enhancing intangibles outlined in this book, then teaching kids the value of collective effort and how their actions can impact the culture of a team will be a useful undertaking. By educating and reinforcing cultural standards, young players will be more likely to understand why developing enhancing intangibles are important within a sport context, but also during future endeavours they choose to pursue outside of sport.

The timing could not be more appropriate for municipal, provincial, or even national organizations to proactively examine the keystones of culture at the grassroots level of hockey. Both the junior and professional levels have recently been scrutinized in regard to the "player environment." Over the last 24 months, as of June 2021, several notable stories have shaken the foundation of structural expectations and tolerance within the game. For example, Matt Larkin wrote an article titled "Culture in Hockey: Progressive Minds Argue Need for Complete Overhaul." This rather strong title appeared within a well-respected media outlet, *The Hockey News*, after a single tweet in November of 2019. The tweet itself was rather innocently written by a long-time professional hockey player who was commenting on the firing of a prominent coach at the NHL level, but the ripple it caused was profound. It is not my place to regurgitate the facts but suffice to say this event provoked a larger conversation about hockey culture including allegations of racist, misogynistic, homophobic, and potentially abusive behaviour that has been silently tolerated within hockey for decades.

In my opinion, there is a clear distinction between the broader systemic culture in question, and the specific organizational culture discussed in this book. While both systemic and organizational culture intersect at some stage, they also widely diverge in many ways. For example, two former players filed a lawsuit against the Canadian Hockey League in June 2020, citing incidents that took place in their early junior hockey careers during the 2002-2003 time frame. One of the cited incidents involved a player, not a part of the lawsuit, that shared a story about his experience with two different organizational cultures within the OHL that underscores the distinction between the overarching systemic and organizational culture. During his interview with David Pszenyczny, Ken Campbell of *The Hockey News* paraphrased a part of that conversation, highlighting the marked difference in atmosphere from one organization to another:

> It created a toxic atmosphere that lasted his entire time in Sarnia. He and Carcillo played two full seasons in Sarnia, then were both traded to the Mississauga IceDogs early in the 2004–05 season. He said it was only when he arrived in Mississauga that he realized what constituted a healthy atmosphere (Campbell, 2020).

Reading the quote was quite a timely revelation, as it captured the marked difference between cultures of two individual organizations competing in the same league. Further, despite a lingering and alleged larger systemic cultural issue within the league at that time, teams can in fact create a "healthy atmosphere," as Pszenyczny stated. A healthy culture should realistically be the goal of any sport organization dealing with young athletes, and in my own experience it needs to start at the top. As previously noted, the leaders of an organization must first decide what great looks like. Once great has been defined, an organization can then clearly communicate desirable intangibles, but also those damaging intangibles they want to avoid as they build their team. This concept can be applied toward junior hockey draft choices, or hiring the right candidates for a blossoming business.

Whether you as a reader agree with the existence of a systemic cultural problem in the game of hockey is a matter of opinion. What I can say is this: as the style in which the game of hockey has evolved (i.e., speed and skill vs. tough and rugged), so too has the underlying culture, and it has had an undeniable influence on the importance placed upon, or definition of any given intangible. Keep in mind, the junior hockey lawsuit outlined above took place during the 2002–03 OHL season. At the professional level, a single tweet in November of 2019 outlined an incident that unfolded while playing in the American Hockey League (the professional minor league level just below the NHL) during the 2009–10 season, created a jolt throughout the league. At both levels, a decade or more had lapsed since either incident had taken place, and the careers of those involved went in all kinds of directions during that time—one player won two Stanley Cups, another player personally suffered, while a different player was seemingly unfazed and was now coaching, and one coach involved was steadily promoted to an NHL head coach position. This is not an attempt to excuse or undermine any of the allegations or incidents, and while I think and hope the underlying culture of hockey has changed for the better during the last decade, there is obviously still a long way to go. As described within the subtheme of enhancing intangibles, the definition of character within hockey from 30 years ago is likely now very different from the variety of definitions that were uncovered throughout this book. I believe these changes have brought about a more positive overall environment for players within the game, meaning the culture of hockey has slowly evolved and improved, but it can always advance further. That is a crucial part of culture in any sense of the word. A strong, successful, sustainable culture should continually be evolving and rarely, if ever, does it stay stagnant. Player intangibles clearly play a factor in the evaluation process of young athletes, and organizations that want to improve or maintain a successful culture should be cognizant of the characteristics, attitudes, and beliefs that symbolize the cultural standards of success within the team. If the identification of intangibles is accepted as a means toward cultural enrichment, then the development of enhancing intangibles should not only become a larger focus for young athletes, but also a key component of the sport experience and curriculum. That means educating, teaching, and reinforcing the benefits of a healthy culture to young players so that they can continue the positive evolution within hockey and within the larger realm of youth sport.

Bibliography

Abbott, A., & Collins, D. (2004). Eliminating the dichotomy between theory and practice in talent identification and development: Considering the role of psychology. *Journal of Sports Sciences, 22*, 395–408. doi:10.1080/02640410410001675324

Aliev, B. (2012). Nail Yakupov Profile. Retrieved from www.mynhldraft. com/2012/NHL-Draft-Profiles/Nail-Yakupov

Anshel, M. H., & Lidor, R. (2012). Talent detection programs in sport: The questionable use of psychological measures. *Journal of Sport Behavior, 35*, 239–266. doi:10.1177/2167479515591789

Baker, J., Schorer, J., Cobley, S., Schimmer, G., & Wattie, N. (2009). Circumstantial development and athletic excellence: The role of date of birth and birthplace. *European Journal of Sport Science, 9*, 329–339. doi:10.1080/17461390902933812

Barnsley R. H., Thompson A. H., & Barnsley P. E. (1985). Hockey success and birthdate: The relative age effect. *Canadian Association of Health, Physical Education and Recreation (CAHPER) Journal, 51*, 23–28.

Bean, C. N., Jeffery-Tosoni, S., Fraser-Thomas, J., & Baker, J. (2016). Negative parental behaviour in Canadian minor hockey: Insiders' perceptions and recommendations. *Revue phénEPS/PHEnex Journal, 7*, 46–67.

Betsch, C. (2008). Chronic preferences for intuition and deliberation in decision making. In H. Plessner, C. Betsch, & T. Betsch (Eds.), *Intuition in judgment and decision making* (pp. 3–22). New York: Erlbaum.

Braun, V., & Clarke, V. (2006). Using thematic analysis in psychology. *Qualitative Research in Psychology, 3*, 77–101. doi:10.1191/1478088706qp063oa

Bueckert, K. (2020, June 16). OHL to investigate former player's allegation of forced drug use. CBC. Retrieved from https://www.cbc.ca/news/canada/kitchener-waterloo/ohl-eric-guest-kitchener-rangers-drug-use-party-1.5614603

Calder, J. M., & Durbach, I. N. (2015). Decision support for evaluating player performance in rugby union. *International Journal of Sports Science & Coaching, 10*, 21–37. doi:10.1260/1747-9541.10.1.21

Chapman, D. S., & Rowe, P. M. (2001). The impact of videoconference technology, interview structure, and interviewer gender on interviewer evaluations in the employment interview: A field experiment. *Journal of Occupational and Organizational Psychology, 74*, 279–298.

Chelladurai, P., & Saleh, S. D. (1978). Preferred leadership in sports. *Canadian Journal of Applied Sport Sciences, 3*, 85–92.

Ciarrochi, J., & Mayer, J. D. (2007). The key ingredients of emotional intelligence interventions: Similarities and differences. In J. Ciarrochi & J. D. Mayer (Eds.), *Applying emotional intelligence: A practitioner's guide* (pp. 144–156). New York: Psychology Press.

Cresswell, S. L., & Eklund, R. C. (2006). The nature of player burnout in rugby: Key characteristics and attributions. *Journal of Applied Sport Psychology, 18*, 219–239. doi:10.1080/10413200600830299

De Dreu, C. K. W., & Weingart, L. R. (2003). Task versus relationship conflict, team performance, and team member satisfaction: A meta-analysis. *Journal of Applied Psychology, 88*, 741–749. doi:10.1037/0021-9010.88.4.741

Dorsch, T. E., King, M. Q., Dunn, C. R., Osai, K. V., & Tulane, S. (2017). The impact of evidence-based parent education in organized youth sport: A pilot study. *Journal of Applied Sport Psychology, 29*, 199–214. doi:10.1080/10413200.2016.1194909

Dohme, L.-C., Backhouse, S., Piggott, D., & Morgan, G. (2017). Categorising and defining popular psychological terms used within the youth athlete talent development literature: A systematic review. *International Review of Sport & Exercise Psychology, 10*, 134–163. doi:10.1080/1750984X.2016.1185451

Elferink-Gemser, M. T., Huijgen, B. C., Coelho-E-Silva, M., Lemmink, K. A., & Visscher, C. (2012). The changing characteristics of talented soccer players – a decade of work in Groningen. *Journal of Sports Sciences, 30*, 1581–1591. doi:10.1080/02640414.2012.725854

Elliott, S. K., & Drummond, M. N. (2017). During play, the break, and the drive home: the meaning of parental verbal behaviour in youth sport. *Leisure Studies, 36*, 645–656. doi:10.1080/02614367.2016.1250804

Falk, B., Lidor, R., Lander, Y., & Lang, B. (2004). Talent identification and early development of elite water-polo players: A 2-year follow-up study. *Journal of Sports Sciences, 22*, 347–355. doi:10.1080/02640410310001641566

Feloni, R. (2015). Google HR boss shares the company's 4 rules for hiring exceptional employees. *Eastern Worker, 55*, 7–9.

Fine, M., Weis, L., Weseen, S., & Wong, L. (2000). For whom? Qualitative research, representations, and social responsibilities. In N. K. Denzin & Y. S. Lincoln (Eds.), *Handbook of qualitative research* (2nd ed., pp. 107–131). Thousand Oaks, CA: Sage.

Francis, J. J., Johnston, M., Robertson, C., Glidewell, L., Entwistle, V., Eccles, M. P., & Grimshaw, J. M. (2010). What is an adequate sample size? Operationalising data saturation for theory-based interview studies. *Psychology & Health, 25*, 1229–1245. doi:10.1080/08870440903194015

García-Izquierdo, A. L., Vilela, L. D., & Moscoso, S. (2015). Work analysis for personnel selection. In I. Nikolaou & J. K. Oostrom (Eds.), *Employee recruitment, selection, and assessment: Contemporary issues for theory and practice* (pp. 9–26). Hove, England: Psychology Press.

Gerrard, B. (2017). The role of analytics in assessing playing talent. In J. Baker, S. Cobley, J. Schorer, & N. Wattie (Eds.), *Routledge handbook of talent identification and development in sport* (pp. 423–431). New York: Routledge.

Hays, D. G., Wood, C., Dahl, H., & Kirk-Jenkins, A. (2016). Methodological rigor in Journal of Counseling & Development qualitative research articles: A 15-year review. *Journal of Counseling & Development, 94,* 172–183. doi:10.1002/jcad.12074

Halliwell, W. (1989). Delivering sport psychology services to the Canadian sailing team at the 1988 summer Olympic Games. *The Sport Psychologist, 3,* 313–319. doi:10.1123/tsp.3.4.313

Hammell, S., & Kleiner, B. (2015). Excellence in teams. *Global Education Journal, 2,* 141–150.

Hockey Canada (2013). *Hockey Canada long term player development plan: Hockey for life, hockey for excellence.* Retrieved from https://www.hockeyalberta.ca/uploads/source/HC_-_LTPD_Manual.pdf

Holt, N. L., & Dunn, J. G. H. (2004). Towards a grounded theory of the psychosocial competencies and environmental conditions associated with soccer success. *Journal of Applied Sport Psychology, 6,* 199–219. doi:10.1080/10413200490437949

Holt, N. L., & Knight, C. J. (2014). *Parenting in sport: From research to practice.* London: Routledge.

Holt, N. L., Knight, C. J., & Zukiwski, P. (2012). Female athletes' perceptions of teammate conflict in sport: Implications for sport psychology consultants. *The Sport Psychologist, 26,* 135–154. doi:10.1123/tsp.26.1.135

Holt, N. L., Neely, K. C., Slater, L. G., Camiré, M., Côté, J., Fraser-Thomas, J., Macdonald, D. J., Strachan, L.,Tamminen, K. A. (2017). A grounded theory of positive youth development through sport based on results from a qualitative meta-study. *International Review of Sport and Exercise Psychology, 10,* 1–49. doi:10.1080/1750984X.2016.1180704

Holt, N. L., Pankow, K., Tamminen, K. A., Strachan, L., MacDonald, D. J., Fraser-Thomas, J., Côté, J., Camiré, M. (2018). A qualitative study of research priorities among representatives of Canadian provincial sport organizations. *Psychology of Sport and Exercise, 36,* 8–16. doi:10.1016/jpsychsport.2018.01.002

ICSA - The Institute of Chartered Secretaries and Administrators (2018). Organisational culture in sport: Assessing and improving attitudes and behaviours. Retrieved from https://www.icsa.org.uk/assets/files/policy/ research/Organisational-culture-in-sport.pdf

Jeffery-Tosoni, S., Fraser-Thomas, J., & Baker, J. (2015). Parent involvement in Canadian youth hockey: Experiences and perspectives of peewee players. *Journal of Sport Behavior, 38,* 3–25.

Kavekar, A. N., & Ford, S. J. (2010). Investigation of recruiting criteria of leading NCAA division I softball coaches. *The Sport Journal, 13,* 1–7.

Kerr, J. (2013). *Legacy: What the All Blacks can teach us about the business of life.* London, England: Constable.

Knight, C. J., Berrow, S. R., & Harwood, C. G. (2017). Parenting in sport. *Current Opinion in Psychology, 16,* 93–97. doi:10.1016/j.copsyc.2017.03.011

Knight, C. J., Neely, K. C., & Holt, N. L. (2011). Parental behaviors in team sports: How do female athletes want parents to behave? *Journal of Applied Sport Psychology, 23,* 76–92. doi:/10.1080/10413200.2010.525589

Koz, D., Fraser-Thomas, J., & Baker, J. (2012). Accuracy of professional sports drafts in predicting career potential. *Scandinavian Journal of Medicine & Science in Sports, 22,* 64–69. doi:10.1111/j.1600-0838.2011.01408.x

Larkin, P., & O'Connor, D. (2017). Talent identification and recruitment in youth soccer: Recruiter's perceptions of the key attributes for player recruitment. *PLOS ONE, 12,* 1–15. doi:10.1080/02640410050120041

Lawless, G. (2013, September 4). Best NHL draft picks have a certain intangible. *Winnipeg Free Press.* Retrieved from http://www.winnipegfreepress.

com/opinion/columnists/best-nhl-draft-picks-have-a-certain-intangible-222299281.html

Lerner, R. M., Lerner, J. V., Lewin-Bizan, S., Bowers, E. P., Boyd, M., Kiely, M., Schmid, K., Napolitano, C. M. (2011). Positive youth development: Processes, programs, and problematics. *Journal of Youth Development, 6,* 38–62. doi:/10.5195/jyd.2011.174

Malloy, S. (2011). *The art of scouting: How the hockey experts really watch the game and decide who makes it.* Mississauga, ON: Wiley.

Malterud, K., Siersma, V. D., & Guassora, A. D. (2016). Sample size in qualitative interview studies. *Qualitative Health Research, 26,* 1753–1760. doi:10.1177/1049732315617444

Markula, P., & Silk, M. (2011). *Qualitative research for physical culture.* London, UK: Palgrave MacMillan.

Marsh, H. W. (1994). Sport motivation orientations: Beware of jingle-jangle fallacies. *Journal of Sport and Exercise Psychology, 16,* 365–380. doi:10.1123/jsep.16.4.365

Martin, L. J., Wilson, J., Evans, M. B., & Spink, K. S. (2015). Cliques in sport: Perceptions of intercollegiate athletes. *The Sport Psychologist, 29,* 82-95. doi:10.1123/tsp.2014-0003

Maykut, P., & Morehouse, R. (1994). *Beginning qualitative research.* Washington, DC: Falmer Press.

Mills, A., Butt, J., Maynard, I., & Harwood, C. (2012). Identifying factors perceived to influence the development of elite youth football academy players. *Journal of Sports Sciences, 30,* 1593-1604. doi:10.1080/02640414.2012.710753

Morgan, P. B., Fletcher, D., & Sarkar, M. (2015). Understanding team resilience in the world's best athletes: A case study of a rugby union World Cup winning team. *Psychology of Sport and Exercise, 16,* 91-100. doi:10.1016/j.psychsport.2014.08.007

Morris, T. (2000). Psychological characteristics and talent identification in soccer. *Journal of Sports Sciences, 18*, 715-726. doi:10.1080/02640410050120096

Neely, K. C., Dunn, J. G. H., McHugh, T.-L., & Holt, N. L. (2016). The deselection process in competitive female youth sport. *The Sport Psychologist, 30*, 141-153. doi:10.1123/tsp.2015-0044

Neergaard, M. A., Olesen, F., Andersen, R. S., & Sondergaard, J. (2009). Qualitative description – the poor cousin of health research? *BMC Medical Research Methodology, 9*, 52. doi:10.1186/1471-2288-9-52

Nieuwenhuis, C. F., Spamer, E. J., & Van Rossum, J. H. (2002). Prediction function for identifying talent in 14- to 15-year-old female field hockey players. *High Ability Studies, 13*, 21-33. doi:10.1080/13598130220132280

O'Sullivan, J. (2017, April 18). The talent that whispers. Retrieved from http://changingthegameproject.com/the-talent-that-whispers/

Pynn, S., Dunn, J. G. H., & Holt, N. L. (in press). A qualitative study of exemplary parenting in competitive female youth sport. *Sport, Exercise, and Performance Psychology*.

Raedeke, T. D. (1997). Is athlete burnout more than just stress? A sport commitment perspective. *Journal of Sport and Exercise Psychology, 19*, 396-417. doi:10.1123/jsep.19.4.396

Rees, T., Hardy, L., Güllich, A., Abernethy, B., Côté, J., Woodman, T., Montgomery, H., Laing, S., Warr, C. (2016). The Great British medalists project: A review of current knowledge on the development of the world's best sporting talent. *Sports Medicine, 46*, 1041–1058. doi:10.1007/s40279-016-0476-2

Reimer, H. A., & Toon, K. (2001). Leadership and satisfaction in tennis: Examination of congruence, gender, and ability. *Research Quarterly for Exercise and Sport, 72*, 243–256.

Ross, A. J., Mallett, C. J., & Parkes, J. F. (2015). The influence of parent sport behaviours on children's development: Youth coach and administrator perspectives. *International Journal of Sports Science & Coaching, 10*, 605–621. doi:10.1260/1747-9541.10.4.605

Rubin, H. J., & Rubin, I. S. (2012). *Qualitative interviewing: The art of hearing data.* Thousand Oaks, CA: Sage.

Salovey, P., & Mayer, J. D. (1990). Emotional intelligence. *Imagination, Cognition, and Personality, 9*, 185–211. doi:0.2190/DUGG-P24E-52WK-6CDG

Sandelowski, M. (2000). Focus on research methods: Whatever happened to qualitative description? *Research in Nursing and Health, 23*, 334–340. doi:10.1002/1098-240X

Sandelowski, M. (2010). What's in a name? Qualitative description revisited. *Research in Nursing and Health, 33*, 77–84. doi:10.1002/nur.20362

Saw, A. E., Main, L. C., Robertson, S., & Gastin, P. B. (2017). Athlete self-report measure use and associated psychological alterations. *Sports (Basel, Switzerland), 5*, 54. doi:10.3390/sports5030054

Schmitt, N., Cortina, J. M., Ingerick, M. J., & Wiechmann, D. (2003). Personnel selection and employee performance. In W. C. Borman, D. R. Ilgen, & R. J. Klimoski (Eds.), *Handbook of psychology (Vol. 12): Industrial and organizational psychology* (pp. 77–105). Hoboken, NJ: Wiley.

Schroeder, P. J. (2010). Changing team culture: The perspectives of ten successful head coaches. *Journal of Sport Behavior, 33*, 63–88.

Schuckers, M., & Argeris, S. (2015). You can beat the market: Estimating the return on investment for National Hockey League (NHL) team scouting using a draft value pick chart for the NHL. *Journal of Sports Analytics, 1*, 111–119. doi:103233/JSA-150015

Smith, B., & McGannon, K. R. (2017). Developing rigor in qualitative research: Problems and opportunities within sport and exercise psychology. *International Review of Sport and Exercise Psychology, 11*, 101–121. doi:10.1080/1750984X.2017.1317357

Solomon, G. B. (2008). The assessment of athletic ability in intercollegiate sport: Instrument construction and validation. *International Journal of Sports Science & Coaching, 3,* 513–525. doi:10.1260/174795408787186477

Solomon, G. B., & Rhea, D. J. (2008). Sources of expectancy information among college coaches: A qualitative test of expectancy theory. *International Journal of Sports Science & Coaching, 3,* 251–268. doi:10.1260/174795408785100725

Spamer, E. J. (2009). Talent identification and development in youth rugby players: A research review. *South African Journal for Research in Sport Physical Education and Recreation, 31,* 109–118. doi:10.4314/sajrs.v31i2.46332

Tamminen, K. A., & Crocker, P. R. (2013). "I control my own emotions for the sake of the team": Emotional self-regulation and interpersonal emotion regulation among female high-performance curlers. *Psychology of Sport & Exercise, 14,* 737–747. doi:10.1016/j.psychsport.2013.05.002

Taylor, J. (1995). A conceptual model for integrating athletes' needs and sport demands in the development of competitive mental preparation strategies. *The Sport Psychologist, 9,* 339–357. doi:10.1123/tsp.9.3.339

Thorne, S. E. (2016). *Interpretive description: Qualitative research for applied practice.* New York: Routledge.

Tingling, P. M. (2017). Educated guesswork: Drafting in the National Hockey League. In J. Albert, M. E. Glickman, T. B. Swartz, & R. H. Koning (Eds.), *Handbook of statistical methods and analyses in sports* (pp. 327–340). Boca Raton, FL: CRC Press.

Uhlmann, E. L., & Barnes, C. M. (2014). Selfish play increases during high-stakes NBA games and is rewarded with more lucrative contracts. *PLOS ONE, 9,* 1–5. doi:10.1371/journal.pone.0095745

Vaeyens, R., Lenoir, M., Williams, A. M., & Phillippaerts, R. M. (2008). Talent identification and development programmes in sport—current models and future directions. *Sports Medicine, 8,* 703–714. doi:10.2165/00007256-200838090-00001

Vallerand, J. V., Mageau, A. G., Elliot, A. J., Dumais, A., Demers, M., & Rousseau, F. (2008). Passion and performance attainment in sport. *Psychology of Sport and Exercise, 3*, 373–392. doi:10.1016/j.psychsport.2007.05.003

Van Yperen, N. W. (2009). Why some make it and others do not: Identifying psychological factors that predict career success in professional adult soccer. *The Sport Psychologist, 23*, 317–329. doi:10.1123/tsp.23.3.317

Verdinelli, S., & Scagnoli, N. I. (2013). Data display in qualitative research. *International Journal of Qualitative Methods, 12*, 359–381. doi:10.1177/160940691301200117

Verner-Filion, J., Vallerand, R. J., Amiot, C. E., & Mocanu, I. (2017). The two roads from passion to sport performance and psychological well-being: The mediating role of need satisfaction, deliberate practice, and achievement goals. *Psychology of Sport and Exercise, 30*, 19–29. doi:10.1016/j.psychsport.2017.01.009

Vollman, R. (2016). *Hockey abstract presents stat shot: The ultimate guide to hockey analytics.* Toronto: ECW Press.

Western Hockey League (2019, June 24). 28 WHL players selected in 2019 NHL Draft. Retrieved from
https://whl.ca/article/28-whl-players-selected-at-2019-nhl-draft

Wegman, J. (2020, April 14). Burke: Yakupov's draft interview worst I've ever had in my life. Sportsnet. Retrieved from https://www.thescore.com/nhl/news/1969942

Whiting, S. W., & Maynes, T. D. (2016). Selecting team players: Considering the impact of contextual performance and workplace deviance on selection decisions in the National Football League. *Journal of Applied Psychology, 101*, 484–497. doi:10.1037/ap10000067

Williams, A. M. (2000). Perceptual skill in soccer: Implications for talent identification and development. *Journal of Sports Sciences, 18*, 737–750. doi:10.1080/02640410050120113

Wilner, B. (2012, April 27). QBs Luck, Griffin now have to prove worthy of draft status. The Spokesman-Review. Retrieved from http://www.spokesman.com/stories/2012/apr/27/qbs-luck-griffin-now-have-to-prove-worthy-of/

Woods, C. T., Joyce, C., & Robertson, S. (2015). What are talent scouts actually identifying? Investigating the physical and technical skill match activity profiles of drafted and non-drafted U18 Australian footballers. *Journal of Science and Medicine in Sport, 19,* 419–423. doi:10.1016/j.jsams.2015.04.013

Appendix A – Interview Guide

Hı [NAME OF SCOUT]. THANKS FOR TAKING THE TIME TO participate in this study which I am using to complete my thesis as part of my MA degree at the University of Alberta. The information you provide in the interview will not only help me complete my degree, but will hopefully be used to further enhance the knowledge base we have in the scouting community to help us evaluate future draft picks in the WHL. As a reminder of the things that were written in the information letter you received, I want to reassure you that you are in no way obligated to participate in this interview or answer any specific questions that I might ask. Your participation is completely voluntary and no one inside or outside of your organization or the league will know if you participated or not. I am recording this interview so that I can go back to your responses in detail once we are finished.

I want to assure you that every effort will be made to ensure your anonymity. If there is anything you say that might identify who you are, I will make sure that you get the opportunity to screen the information before it is included in the final version of my thesis or in any public presentation of the study that might follow (e.g., paper or conference presentation). A fake name will be assigned to your interview responses to further protect your identity and to protect the identity of your club and/or anyone who you might mention by name in the interview. Although my supervisory committee members—Dr. John Dunn and Dr. Nick Holt—are co-investigators on this project, it is important to understand that even they will be unable to determine your identity at any stage during the research process. They will never receive a list of the names of the scouts who participate in the study, and they will never have access to the audiotape of this interview. They will have access to the transcripts that come from these interviews, but all of your identifying information (including your name) will be removed from the typed transcripts they eventually receive. So, every effort will be made to ensure that no one knows your identity at every stage of the research.

It's important for me to stress that there are no right or wrong answers to the questions I'm going to ask. As a fellow scout in the league, I'm interested in your experiences, perceptions, and views about the so-called "intangible player characteristics" that you use to evaluate players and that you consider in your decision-making process as to whether or not you think a player would make a good draft prospect. The things I'm talking about go beyond the physical, technical, and tactical abilities that scouts typically consider when evaluating players. These intangible player characteristics are often harder to see, harder to evaluate, and harder to describe than many of the physical, technical, and tactical abilities that we consider, but are still considered by scouts as being important when making our draft-selection choices.

So, the focus of this interview is based around your views of what these intangible player characteristics are, and why you think they are important to consider when making decisions about draft prospects. They can relate directly to the player or anything that you consider to be part of the player's background.

Now that I've given you an overview of why we are having this interview, do you have any questions you want to ask me before we get started?

INTRODUCTORY QUESTIONS

Just to get us started, and for a bit of background information (which we will not include in the published report), can you tell me about your own previous competitive experiences in sport, and a bit about your background as an amateur scout in the league?

Probes:
- Were you ever drafted by a junior or professional team?
- Did you end up playing in that league?
- How did you get involved in scouting?
- How long have you been scouting in the WHL?

- How many teams have you scouted for in the league?
- What is your official title within your organization?
- Is scouting your full-time position?
- Approximately how many games do you scout in a typical WHL season?
- How many WHL drafts have you attended?
- At what age did you first begin scouting for a WHL organization?

Before we talk about the "intangible characteristics of players" that you consider important, can you briefly tell me about some of the more obvious (or objective) player characteristics that you typically evaluate when you assess a player?

Probes:
- Physical?
- Tactical?
- Technical?
- Game sense?
- Performance indicators? (analytics and game statistics)
- How difficult is it to typically assess these characteristics?
- What do you think the typical level of consensus or agreement would be among the WHL scouting community if you all sat down and watched the same player at the same time on five different occasions throughout a season?

MAIN QUESTIONS

Now that you have given me your thoughts on what we might call the more obvious or objective player characteristics that you evaluate, let's turn our attention to the more intangible characteristics that you consider when you evaluate potential draft prospects. As I said earlier, these are things that may be harder to see, harder to evaluate, or harder to describe, and usually go beyond the technical, tactical, and physical attributes of players, but are things about a player you'd like to know or feel are important to know before you draft him.

What Question(s): Can you please list and describe the intangible player characteristics (beyond the physical, technical, and tactical abilities of players) that you consider when you evaluate players for the draft?

Probes:
- Why is each characteristic important?
- How easy or difficult is it for you or your organization to obtain information about these characteristics?

Why Question(s): How much do intangible characteristics weigh into decisions when making draft choices?

Probes:
- Are these characteristics formally or informally evaluated and discussed within your organization?
- How much time is spent discussing these characteristics within your organization at the draft?
- Does the importance of intangibles vary as a function of higher vs. lower ranked/rated prospects? Do intangibles influence the order of your teams' draft list?

Question: If you had a player who possessed all of the necessary physical, technical, and tactical abilities to be successful as a hockey player in your organization, are there any intangible characteristics that a player might possess (or not possess), or that exist in the player's background, that would make you very reluctant to draft him?

Probes:
- Why?
- Has this ever been a determining factor in deciding not to draft a player? (Provide details if such a case exists.)

Question: Can you think of any cases within your organization (or within another organization) where more knowledge or more consideration of certain intangible characteristics of a player might have influenced a team's decision to draft (or not draft) the player?

- Probe for specific good/bad examples of players

Question: Can you think of any cases within your organization (or within another organization) where a player was not considered to have the physical, technical, or tactical abilities to be successful, but the player was nevertheless drafted as a result of the intangible characteristics he possessed, and went on to be successful in your team or in the league?

- Probe for specific good/bad examples of players

How Questions(s): Can you please list and describe how you gather information on intangible player characteristics (beyond the physical, technical, and tactical abilities of players) that you consider when you evaluate players for the draft?

- How/where/when do you gather this information?
- Who do you talk to get this information? (Coaches, parents, teachers, social media, interviews, questionnaires?)

Do you have any specific examples of sources that provide or added more insightful data than others?

Question: If you were to select the three most important intangible player characteristics that you would advise young players to develop to enhance their prospects of being drafted, what would they be?

- Why did you select these three examples?

CLOSING QUESTION

Is there anything else about the intangible characteristics of players or the way we evaluate or consider these attributes in our draft-selection evaluations that we have not yet discussed but you would like to mention before we end the interview?

Appendix B – Member Reflection One Page Summary and Graphic

THE PURPOSE OF THIS STUDY WAS TO IDENTIFY "INTANGIBLE player characteristics" that junior scouts used to determine the draft suitability of eligible hockey players in the Western Hockey League. The findings suggest that after scouts identify players with adequate on-ice playing ability, they then sought more information about the person behind the player. The perception of the person was reflected by scouts' evaluation of two different types of intangibles—intangibles that enhanced players draft status and intangibles that diminished players draft status. Enhancing intangibles were seen to increase the draft status of a player and included *compete, character, leadership/being a team player,* and *passion.* Diminishing intangibles, which often raised red flags for scouts, were seen to decrease the draft status of a player and included a *lack of enhancing intangibles, bad body language, selfish behaviour,* and undesirable *parental behaviour.* When junior hockey scouts prepared the final list of player names for the annual WHL draft, their final decision between players with similar playing ability often came down to the intangibles (enhancing vs. diminishing intangibles) of those players. More specifically, when scouts were forced into making decisions about a group of similar players, they used intangibles to choose the player that best fit the current organizational culture. Junior hockey teams wanted to incorporate players, especially after the first several rounds, that were good, well-rounded citizens representing the team or brand in a positive fashion, as opposed to selecting a player that might be disruptive to the organization in the future.

Especially after the elite players (in terms of physical playing ability) were selected in the first several rounds, scouts appeared to prefer the best person, according to intangibles important to the organization, over the physical ability of a player (see display graphic).

Display Graphic:

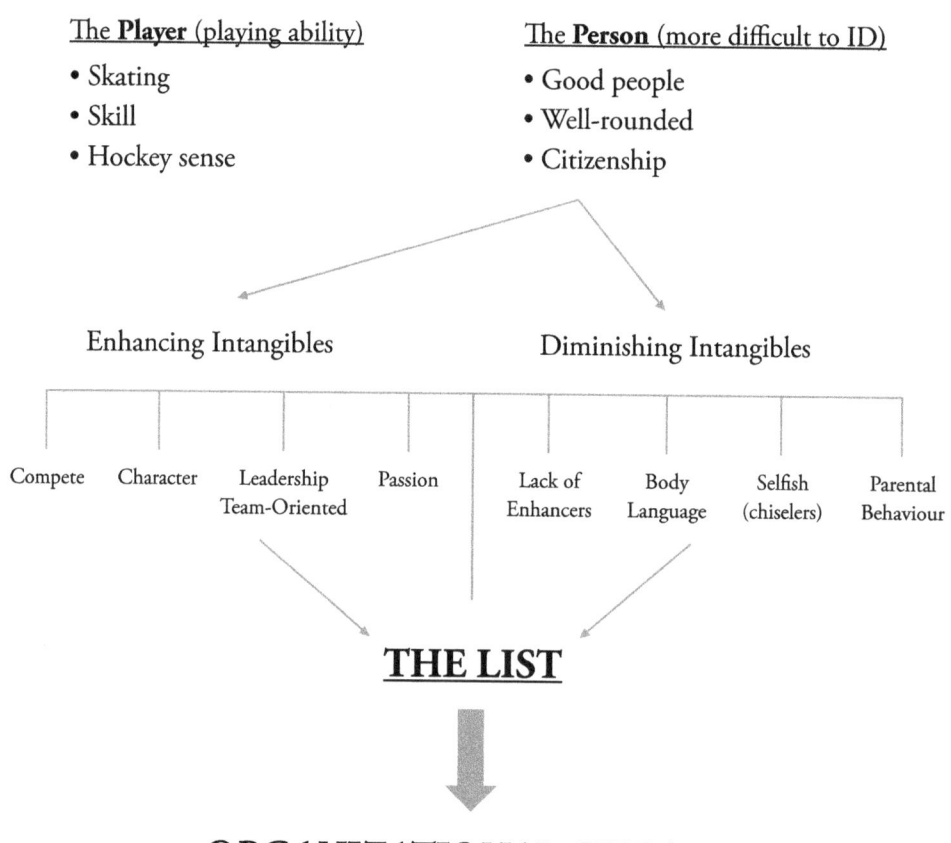

The **Player** (playing ability)

- Skating
- Skill
- Hockey sense

The **Person** (more difficult to ID)

- Good people
- Well-rounded
- Citizenship

Enhancing Intangibles

Diminishing Intangibles

| Compete | Character | Leadership Team-Oriented | Passion | | Lack of Enhancers | Body Language | Selfish (chiselers) | Parental Behaviour |

THE LIST

ORGANIZATIONAL CULTURE

CPSIA information can be obtained
at www.ICGtesting.com
Printed in the USA
BVHW040255080921
616193BV00006B/123